Turn
Your

Dreams
Into

Reality

About the Author

Gini Graham Scott, PhD, JD, is a nationally known writer, consultant, speaker, and seminar leader specializing in business and work relationships, professional and personal development, social trends, popular culture, and lifestyles. She has published over fifty books on diverse subjects, and is a regular *Huffington Post* columnist, commenting on social trends, new technology, business, and everyday life. Her websites include www.ginigrahamscott.com and www.changemakerspublishingandwriting.com.

She is the founder of Changemakers Publishing, which features books on self-help, work, business, psychology, and social trends. She has published over forty print on demand and e-books, and has licensed several dozen books for foreign sales in the UK, Russia, Korea, Spain, and Japan. She is also the Director of Publishers Agents and Films (www.publishersagentsandfilms.com), which connects writers and filmmakers to publishers, agents, and the film industry.

She has received national media exposure for her books, including appearances on *Good Morning America*, the *Oprah Winfrey Show*, the *Montel Williams Show*, and CNN. Her books on business relationships and professional development include *A Survival Guide for Working with Humans*, *Working with Bad Bosses*, and *Managing the Employee from Hell*. Her books on social trends and popular culture include *Scammed*, *The New Middle Ages*, *Internet Book Piracy*, *Lies and Liars: How and Why Sociopaths Lie*, and *The Very Next New Thing*.

Gini has also been the producer and host of a talk show series, CHANGEMAKERS, featuring interviews on social trends.

Turn Your Dreams Into Reality

Simple Techniques to Get What You Want

Gini Graham Scott, PhD

Llewellyn Publications
Woodbury, Minnesota

First Edition
First Printing, 2015

Cover art by iStockphoto.com/44253142 /©cat_arch_angel
Cover design by Ellen Lawson
Interior art by iStockphoto.com/44253142 /©cat_arch_angel
Editing by Jennifer Ackman

Llewellyn Publications is a registered trademark of Llewellyn Worldwide Ltd.

Library of Congress Cataloging-in-Publication Data (Pending)
ISBN: 978-0-7387-4529-9

Llewellyn Publications
A Division of Llewellyn Worldwide Ltd.
2143 Wooddale Drive
Woodbury, MN 55125-2989
www.llewellyn.com

Printed in the United States of America

Other Books by This Author

Contents

Exercise List

Below is a list of exercises, the estimated time to complete them, and their page number.

Introduction

For the last three decades I have been working with the Get What You Want (GWYW) approach to life, which is based on clearly determining what you want, envisioning it, and then getting it. Most recently I used this to decide where I wanted to move, what kind of house I wanted, which part of town, and what I hoped to pay. Then after looking at one house that fit the bill, I quickly decided where I wanted to be. Four weeks later that's exactly where I moved. I have used this same technique to target houses, work, and other goals in the past. So it's a time-tested approach that I have used myself and in numerous workshops as well.

Essentially, this approach consists of three simple steps:

1) You determine what you really want—and can realistically obtain.

2) You see a clear vision of what you want and see yourself achieving that.

3) You take the needed steps to get it, including overcoming any obstacles, making any modifications, and finally, enjoying the experience of achieving what you want.

As you take these steps, you see your goal and the needed steps or modifications in your mind—so your power of visualization is essentially your guide to gaining what you desire.

The ability to visualize, or mentally imagine, what you want and what you need to do to get there is like your car engine and steering wheel combined. You rev it up and then drive exactly where you want to go, making changes in your route as need be. By clearly visualizing what you want, you tap into your creative energy which helps to propel you to your goal and know what to do in order to get there. Plus, you can draw on images and ideas that are already meaningful and powerful for you, such as calling on a spiritual teacher, guide, or imagined real-life mentor to help with wisdom and support. Or you can create new images and ideas you associate with things you want to achieve your goals.

Tapping into Your Mind Power or Creative Force

The first part of this book deals with how to tap into your mind powers and the following sections deal with how to apply them to get what you want in different areas of your life. As you'll discover in part one, these powerful techniques will help you access the inner powers of your mind, use them to empower yourself to get what you want, and to feel more satisfaction at work and in your personal life. You can use these powers for everything from being more successful at work or in business to improving relationships and having more fun. Everyone can use these techniques because everyone has the GWYW abilities. You just have to learn to tap into them and then practice using them until they become second nature.

They will help you:

- Feel more powerful, and as you get in touch with your own power you can do more of what you want to do.

- Increase your confidence and self-esteem as you discover yourself getting the results you want.

- Develop a greater sense of personal identity and purpose as you clarify your direction and goals, and generally find everything working better in your life.

- Be more satisfied with what you are doing and who you are.

- Get more enjoyment out of everyday life—including routine activities and experiences that might otherwise cause upset and stress.

- Tap into your inner radar and sense of knowing, which will help you make better choices and better use these techniques.

- Adjust your energy level for optimum functioning, such as by speeding up or slowing down when you want to, overcoming fatigue with an extra energy burst, and discovering a happy balance in how you use your energy.

- Maximize your talents and increase your skills and creativity.

- Design the person you want to be by creating the personality or self-image you want, making you more aware of who you want to be and giving you the tools to become that person.

- Become smarter by sharpening your intellectual powers and memory skills.

- Increase your powers of perception and awareness so you pay more attention and make better use of that information.

- Make better decisions and improve your ability to solve problems because you gain more insight about the issue and what you want to achieve.

- Set specific, achievable goals and attain them.

- Optimize relationships because you are better able to understand others and able to communicate with them.

- Improve your health and eliminate bad habits no matter what the goal—whether you want to lose weight, stop smoking, reduce anxiety, feel better generally, or help the healing process.

- Turn your problems into possibilities—the flip side of every problem is a possibility, and you can make that transformation by seeing each problem as a stepping-stone or learning experience, and then using your inner powers to imagine alternatives and choose the best option.

How to Best Use This Book

To get the best results from this book read the first few chapters for an overview about what the creative force is, how to access it, and best ways to use it. Think about what you would most like to gain from using these techniques and look at the chapters that deal with that topic. You'll also find a list of exercises after the table of contents.

Use the exercises in each chapter to focus on your priorities and select the exercises that are most applicable to your situation. The approximate times listed for some exercises are just guidelines. You may do these exercises more quickly or may prefer to spend more time than suggested. You can determine what suits your situation best. Use the charts and forms with many of the exercises to record your insights and ideas during or after the exercise. They will help you focus on your choices and alternatives, and guide you to the next step. Spend ten to twenty minutes a day working with these techniques to stay in practice. Make them a familiar, comfortable part of your everyday life. Keep a record of what you do. Review any charts and comments every so often to see what you have accomplished.

Most importantly, recognize that these GWYW techniques will help you become more aware, perceptive, and better able to respond appropriately in any situation so you will be better able to do what's best for you and get what you want.

Part One

Tapping Into the Power of GWYW

Chapter One

༄

The Dynamics of the GWYW Techniques

This chapter is designed to show you how these techniques work and the importance of listening to your inner intuition or creative vision for insights, decision making, and increasing your powers of perception and understanding. For example, besides using these techniques to select where I will live or the house I will live in, I have used these techniques to guide me into the film industry, find a business partner, come up with ideas for new books, and most recently, connect with a woman looking for a writing partner to help her with clients building brands for themselves. At any point along the way, these developments might not have happened had I not been open and receptive to them.

How These Techniques Work

These GWYW techniques work because they help you to be more in touch with your intuition, inner voice, true self, or whatever you want to call this. It's a very powerful force within you. This force is often covered up, downplayed, or discounted in modern society because we value being rational and making decisions in a logical way. For example, lawyers, judges, business people, scientists, engineers, and politicians—most of the leaders of our society—are praised for their ability to come up with rational decisions.

While such approaches are fine and necessary for much of modern living, we can also tap into our intuitive and irrational side to gain insights and understandings. When these are combined with rational techniques or used alone, they can help us make even better decisions and choices. This intuitive part of ourselves is linked to our ability to use mental imagery or visualization—functions that are associated with the operations of the right hemisphere of the brain. The right side of the brain has a holistic mode of perceiving information, whereas the left hemisphere uses a logical, linear mode to reason things out. This holistic style is associated with creativity, visual imagery, dreams, feelings, symbols, and synthesis, in contrast to the more linear style associated with mathematics, writing, language, and analysis.

In turn, scientists have been able to pinpoint when people are using this intuitive, image making part of the brain using PET scans, fMRIs, and other brain imaging techniques. These tests show a higher blood flow to the visual cortex, located in the back of the brain, when people work on tasks involving visual imagery.[1] So there are real physical correlations to what you mentally imagine, or visualize, that are shown by the different parts of your brain that become activated.

These mind power techniques are designed to release and develop this inner force within us, which has an incredible power to help us gain all of the benefits we want. Some of these include:

- Setting goals and attaining them
- Increasing your skills and creativity
- Feeling more confident, self-assured, and having higher self-esteem

---

1. Margaret W. Matlin, *Cognition: 6th Edition* (New York: J. Wiley & Sons, 2005), 228.

- Creating the personality and self-image you want
- Gaining insight into others to improve relationships and to be more persuasive in them
- Motivating others
- Solving problems and making decisions
- Raising and lowering your energy level
- Improving your health and eliminating bad habits

This inner force helps us attain these benefits, as it operates powerfully in two main modes. The first is in a receptive mode, which helps you tune in to that inner knowledge and understanding that you don't pick up rationally. The second is an active mode, which allows you to put into action the insights you have gained from that information. You can use this information to shape yourself, influence others, and affect events. Most GWYW techniques emphasize a combination of these modes, but there are some that do emphasize one mode or the other. For example, in using these techniques to set goals, you first use your receptive powers to gain insights about what you want and need. Then, based on these insights, you establish your goals, prioritize them, and set up a system for achieving what you want.

Commonly, this intuitive perception operates through your ability to create images, visualizations, or pictures in your head, which is a skill that everyone possesses or can develop to some degree. Some people prefer to tune in to this inner voice by listening to the words or their inner thoughts, while others tend to respond more to feelings or sensations. Use what works best for you. However, since the visual and auditory modes of perception are most common, the techniques described in this book draw more heavily on the ability to use images or thoughts to tap into this power of the mind. In turn, as you work with these techniques, you'll develop these abilities.

Becoming Aware of and Facilitating
Your Inner Radar

To use this inner knowledge, you first have to notice it and pay attention to it. Once you do and start recognizing when it is accurate and when to act on it, it is an extremely valuable tool for getting what you want. It can help you determine whether or not to trust someone at work or in a relationship, to decide whether to enter into a deal, take a job, or become more serious in a dating relationship. If you listen to these inner insights and respond correctly you can create better work opportunities, better personal relationships, and better chances in whatever you do in life. You have to get in touch with this intuitive and creative part of yourself, and when you learn to perceive this creative force directly, it can be a source of great information and energy.

The Danger of Not Listening
to Your Creative Force

This intuitive energy is not only a signal to help you to get what you want. It can also serve as a warning to avoid something or someone, such as Henrietta experienced when she ignored some inner warning triggers.

It was about 8:30 one fall evening and Henrietta was leaving her office on her way to her car, which was parked a few blocks away. It was a drizzly night and there weren't many people on the dark streets. She saw four kids turn a corner onto her street about a hundred feet away and a sudden tingling sensation urged her to be cautious. For a moment she was tempted to walk on the other side of the street, but she heard a more logical, reassuring voice override this signal saying *But they're just kids ... It's early ... There are other people out ... Don't act afraid by crossing the street ... If you just keep walking with confidence nothing will happen.* The thoughts came quickly and she kept going. After she passed the first pair of kids without incident she thought everything was fine. But just as she passed the second pair an arm reached out, knocked her down, and grabbed her purse.

Fortunately, Henrietta wasn't hurt, but the experience taught her the importance of paying attention and listening to that inner signal and responding accordingly. What Henrietta's story illustrates is that your inner force can act like a kind of early warning signal. Responding to it can increase your chances of a favorable outcome, and not responding can increase the chances of running into problems. So as you learn to get in touch with this inner force it's important to listen to what it is telling you to do, and don't let your inner editor push this signal aside. If you get a strong, clear signal, listen to it and act accordingly.

Knowing When to Use
Your Intuitive, Creative Force

Your mind's intuitive abilities can be a powerful tool if you develop and pay attention to them. Once you are able to tap into them, they are like a beacon lighting the way to a clear path ahead or pointing out the dangers along the way. They are signaling where to go, what problems to avoid, or what to do to prepare to successfully cope with and overcome the difficulties in your path. As you learn how to access this part of your mind using the GWYW techniques described in this book, you will find countless ways to draw on these enhanced powers and apply them to all aspects of your life.

It is important to do the following four things to access and use your inner creative force effectively:

1) Know that you have this intuitive, creative power within you and that you can use it to guide you.

2) Pay attention when you feel a sense of knowing, energy, or urgency rising within you in whatever form it comes to you—as a voice, in pictures, in feelings, or in sensations.

3) Notice what this force is urging you to do.

4) Respond according to the way you feel this energy directing you, whether it is to go after what you want even more energetically, or to stay away.

These methods are something anyone can master. They're not mysterious or magical. They're based on sound, psychological principles describing how the intuitive right-brained power within you operates so you function more effectively and can better create the reality you want.

The Development of These Techniques

I have been developing and using these GWYW techniques for more than forty years. They have become such an automatic part of my life that I use them without thinking about them. Beginning in the mid-1980s I have received even further confirmation of the success of these techniques in my own life and in the latest research about the new techniques to enhance brain functioning.

I started using these methods in 1968 when I began designing games. I used the pictures in my mind to develop game ideas. This exploration began when I organized a game group, which I started because I loved playing games as a child. After starting this group I soon began having occasional dreams about games. A friend suggested hypnosis to come up with more ideas rather than waiting for random dreams, and he led me on my first guided journey into the intuitive part of my mind. I saw all kinds of games in the Macy's toy department. I began creating hundreds of games this way and found publishers for dozens of them.

In the beginning I needed the formal technique of going into an altered hypnotic state with him guiding me and then doing it myself. After awhile I no longer needed any preparatory techniques to relax and could instantly access my imagination, not only for designing games but also for other creative projects. Then I began to apply this method to making decisions and choices in my life, such as what career path to take and what to say to get the job. This led me to become an assistant professor in Georgia and to later get a doctorate in sociology at the University of California, Berkeley, where I studied several spiritual and personal growth groups, which used some similar techniques to further self-development. I later supplemented my explorations with these techniques by attending dozens of workshops on developing creativity, working with hypnosis, using visualization and imagery, exploring consciousness, and meditating, all designed to expand the power of the mind. I kept testing what I learned through my own experiences and I kept further refining these techniques. These techniques are literally integrated with what I do, so I use them automatically along with gathering and processing facts about a particular situation, which I take into consideration in using these intuitive processes.

Applying the GWYW Techniques in Your Own Life

The GWYW techniques in this book are the methods I have found effective in tapping into this inner creative force. Use the same methods as they are described or adapt them by changing the imagery to suit your own style. The key to success with these techniques is to use a series of procedures and symbols to make yourself receptive to contacting the inner force within you. Adapt these basic procedures and techniques so they work for you. Then, once you are in contact with this inner intuitive force, actively mobilize it to achieve your desired goals.

In doing so, use this basic three-step process to propel you along in getting what you want:

1) Be aware and receptive to notice the inner creative power within however it communicates with you—through seeing, hearing, feeling, knowing, or a combination of these.

2) Consider how to respond to the knowledge and insights you have gained, such as by thinking of and assessing different options to decide what you want to do.

3) Take action. Draw on your inner creative powers to act to achieve your desired goals, or avoid any difficulties or barriers you have perceived.

Getting the Most from the GWYW Techniques

Here are some ways to use these techniques to get what you want and you may think of others. In the chart on page 15 you'll see a list of general benefits you might want, along with an example on how to get them. In the area below the example write down how you might apply a particular benefit to your situation.

Another way to use this chart is to think of a specific result you want and then think of the things you need to do or change about yourself to get it. For example, maybe you want to create a new career for yourself in a different field. You might need to have more energy so you can do the work you are currently doing while you develop that new career, increase your confidence to convince people in the new field you can do the job, overcome uncertainty so you are sure it is what you want to do, improve your talents to effectively do the tasks required, or reshape your personality to better suit your new job.

Likewise, if you want to improve your appeal in relationships you might apply these same actions to that end. As you empower yourself through tapping your inner creativity, you will not only find many specific ways to apply the general benefits from these techniques, but you can also set specific goals to achieve and work backward from them to determine what you need to do to reach that goal.

How the GWYW Method Can Help You

General Desires	Examples of Specific Wants or Goals
Overcome stress and relax	Get through a series of deadlines
Have more energy or overcome fatigue	Be alert at an important meeting
Feel more confident and have more self-esteem	Make a good impression at an interview
Overcome negative behavior patterns and blocks	Change behaviors making another angry
Overcome uncertainty or decide what to do	Get over fear of making wrong choice
Recognize the possibilities	Break a logjam with other alternatives
Discover a new direction for yourself	Choose the right career path
Make the best decision	Decide whether to move or not
Set goals and determine the best steps to achieve them	Plan the steps for selling a new product
Turn around a difficult situation	Change an enemy into a friend
Improve and perfect your talents	Become a successful speaker
Shape your desired personality or self-image	Become more outgoing to get a job
Become the best of who you are	Become an even better salesperson
Better understand others for better relationships	Recognize what someone really likes and dislikes to get along better
Sense whether to trust others or not	Decide if the business deal is for real
Recognize the cues that motivate others	Find ways to make your boss say yes
Discover the solutions to problems	Discover how to make more money
Find ways to profit from your problems	See a money-making idea in a problem

Preparing to Use the GWYW Techniques

Using these techniques will eventually become second nature so you won't need any preparatory methods to activate them. You will eventually just switch into intuitive mode, like clicking a channel on your TV remote.

Initially, though, you will have to set the stage in order to trigger the appropriate receptive or active mode. Then, after you have gone through enough rehearsals, these techniques will come automatically when you want them.

There are four key steps to getting properly prepared:

1) Be aware of how your intuitive powers operate so you can get more information and insights from these techniques

2) Schedule some regular time each day to practice

3) Choose a good setting for your practice

4) Relax when you begin using a method that is comfortable for you

In addition, it is helpful to have a notebook, tape, tablet, or recorder to document your ideas and insights.

Knowing Your Own Mind

Recognizing how your mind operates will help you know when to trust and when to act on your insights from these techniques. This is because everyone's mental processes work differently based on a combination of four key ways of receiving information. Some people are more visually oriented so they take in most of their information by seeing pictures. Some are more auditory and take in information primarily by words or thoughts. Others get strong feelings or sensations so they feel something is right or wrong. Still others have a sense of knowing that something is correct or not. We all have abilities in each of these four areas, just to varying degrees. Furthermore, we can improve our powers in each area by working with them.

Thus, you will probably find your ability to see and listen increase as you use the techniques in this book. However, to use these methods most effectively, first judge where you are now so you know where you want to develop and can better assess the knowledge and ideas you get through these techniques. Then you can decide when and how to act appropriately. The following techniques will give you the insight into how you primarily perceive and receive information.

Discovering How You Perceive and Receive Information

Try this exercise to learn how you receive information. Close your eyes and think of the first idea that comes to mind. Do you see it? Hear it? Sense or feel it? Know it? Or does the idea appear in several ways simultaneously? However it comes to you, this is your creative intuition at work in the form you typically perceive and experience it. Whatever way you receive information and ideas is fine. Just be aware of how you do it.

Continue with this exercise a few more times for confirmation and additional insights into yourself. Again close your eyes and wait for the first idea to pop into your mind. Once more notice how the information has come to you. Then ask yourself, *Did the idea appear to me in the same way as it did before? Or did I use another way of perceiving it this time?*

After you have tried this technique four or five times you'll have a better sense of how you perceive messages. For example, you may be consistent in the way you receive information, or your mode of perception may vary extensively so you can readily use different modes. This information can also help you decide if you need to further develop your abilities in one area, or if you want to work toward having more of a balance. If all of your perceptions have been visual or auditory, you may want to increase your ability to trust your intuitive sense of knowing.

Measuring Your Intuitive Abilities

To discover how strong your mind power abilities are in each of these four areas—visual, auditory, sensing, and knowing—use your creative intuition to tell you. Subsequently, you can call on this inner force to track the development of each of your abilities over time.

To rate yourself, close your eyes, get relaxed, and with a piece of paper and pencil at hand, ask yourself, *How strong are my visual abilities on a scale of zero to one hundred?* Notice the first number that pops into your head and write it down.

Next ask yourself *How strong are my auditory abilities on a scale of zero to one hundred?* Again, notice the first number that appears and record it. Do the same thing for your sensing or feeling abilities and for your knowing abilities. This test will give you an overall assessment of how high you are operating in each area. If you track your results, and review them from time to time, you'll see how you are doing in developing your abilities. You'll find that your inner voice or vision doesn't lie. Listen to it and it will give you an accurate picture of how you perceive and receive sensory input and insights.

Scheduling a Regular Time Period for Practice

When you start getting in touch with your creative intuition and working with these techniques, set aside some time for regular practice just as you would in developing any other skill like writing, typing, or playing tennis. Once you learn the basics and begin using these techniques regularly, you can incorporate them into what you do each day so you may not need any special practice time. As with any other skill, the more consistently you work with these techniques and the more you apply them, the more skilled you become.

To get started, plan on about twenty to thirty minutes for practice each day. Use this time to work on achieving the goals you have set for yourself so your practice will help you get what you want. These goals can be anything as long as they are realistic and achievable, such as feeling less stress at work, improving your computer skills, or getting the money you need to buy a new car.

You'll find that, even when you first start practicing, the results will be dramatic. Sometimes you may notice an immediate difference or the change may take a few days, depending on the skill or goal you are trying to achieve. Just pay attention to what is happening in your life, and you'll find the time investment to develop these skills well worth the effort.

Choosing a Good Setting to Practice

Although you can use these techniques anywhere—even on a busy street to tune out annoying noises and distractions—it is best to begin in a quiet place where you can be alone. If some friends or associates want to learn these techniques with you, arrange for a place to practice together. Choose a place that is free of disruptions such as doorbells or ringing phones. If either is not a possibility, leave a note on the door stating you are busy now or turn off your phone. Having a quiet place at first is important so you can learn to focus and direct your attention. Also, using a regular place to practice helps condition you so you are in the appropriate frame of mind to work on these techniques whenever you enter the area. Designating a particular space is much like having an office or studio for certain kinds of work. You know when you're there it is time to work, so you settle down quickly and do what needs to be done.

It also helps to adjust the lighting or use appropriate props depending on what you want to do. For instance, if you want a soothing, calming effect or a setting for deep thinking, low lighting can help create a feeling of calm and quiet. Conversely, if you want to raise your energy for some project or event, strong lighting can help create a more stimulating mood.

If possible, use an object that reinforces your purpose in doing these exercises. Say you want to close a stock deal. Perhaps place a newspaper with stock quotes, a stock certificate, or your presentation folder in front of you so you can concentrate on it. If you want a raise, imagine a pile of money before you. If you want an improved relationship with someone, put a picture of that person before you. You can use anything for a reinforcer. The key is to select a focus that has a relevant meaning for your intended goal.

Getting Relaxed

Whenever you use any GWYW technique, it's important to start off by getting relaxed so you can focus your attention on whatever you want to achieve with that technique. Even if you want to raise your energy to perform an activity, you still have to start in a relaxed state of mind so you can get that one-pointed focus.

Sit in a comfortable position so you are not only ready to relax but also ready to take some action after you attain a relaxed state. Although some people like to lie down to achieve a deeper feeling of relaxation, I prefer the sitting-action mode and am less likely to fall asleep. Close your eyes if you wish.

If you use a sitting position, I recommend sitting straight up on a chair with both feet touching the floor and your hands up or together. This is a comfortable position and you can use it almost anywhere—in an office chair, in a soft living room armchair, or even on a bus or airplane. Keep your spine straight and rest your feet on the floor so you feel solidly grounded. At the same time, hold your hands in front of you with the palms up, or place your hands together with your index fingers and thumbs pointing up and touching so you feel receptive to your feelings and intuitions. If you hold your hands in this special way, they can become a trigger to remind you that you are now tapping into your inner voice. In time you won't need a special trigger because you will internalize the process. But in the beginning these hand positions will help you get in the appropriate mind-set to be receptive. Finally, be sure you are sufficiently warm when you do these exercises. Nothing distracts like feeling chilled.

The following relaxation exercises will help you calm down and get prepared for whatever else you want to do. Work with them at first in your quiet place until you feel comfortable with them. Then you can do them anywhere; you just may have to concentrate harder. These exercises use three calming approaches: focusing on your breath to shift your attention from the distractions and stresses of the outer world to the peaceful inner world, quieting your body to quiet your mind, and concentrating on a soothing visual image or sound to calm both body and mind. Use whatever approach suits you best or combine them if you wish. Either read the instructions as a general guideline or read them aloud as you record them and play back the recording as you follow the instructions.

Focus on Your Breath

Use breathing to help you relax.

Begin by paying attention to your breathing. Notice your breath going in and out, in and out. Experience the different parts of your body moving up and down and in and out as you breathe.

With each breath, direct your breath to a different point in your body. Breathe down to your foot, to your hand, and feel your breath flowing in and out.

Now, consciously breathe slowly and deeply for ten breaths. As you do, repeat to yourself, *I am relaxed. I am relaxed.*

You should now be relaxed. To relax even more, continue using this or another relaxation exercise.

Quiet Your Body

Use muscle tension and a feeling of warmth to calm down.

To begin, tighten all your muscles as tightly as you can. Clench your fists, feet, arms, legs, and stomach muscles. Clench your teeth. Scrunch up your face. Tense everything, then release and relax all your muscles as much as possible. Let everything go and be aware of the difference. Do this three times.

Now, beginning with your feet and working your way up to your head, concentrate on each body part getting warm and relaxed. As you do, say to yourself, *My (toes, feet, legs, thighs, etc.) are now warm and relaxed.* Do this sequentially for each body part.

As you do this, you may become aware of tensions or tightness in certain body areas. If so, you can send healing energy to that part of your body.

Continue relaxing each body part in turn. After you have relaxed your head, conclude the exercise by saying to yourself, *Now I am totally calm, totally relaxed, totally ready to experience whatever comes.*

Concentrate on a Calming Image or Sound

Use images and sounds to slow yourself down. There are many calming images and sounds on which you can concentrate. Below are just a few possibilities.

Visualize yourself entering an elevator. Push one of the buttons to descend. As you pass each floor, you become more and more relaxed. When you are fully relaxed, step out of the elevator feeling calm and refreshed.

Visualize yourself by the seashore. Notice the waves and watch them flow in and out, in and out, in and out. As they do, feel yourself becoming calmer and calmer. Then, when you feel fully calm, leave the shore.

Chant a single syllable or sound like *om* or *ah*. As you do this, experience the sound expanding in your head, erasing all other distracting images and thoughts.

Keeping Records of What You See

As you use these techniques for insights and ideas, you will find it useful to write this information down or record it. There are several advantages to doing this. You won't forget important ideas you get, you can keep track of your development in achieving what you want, or you can chart your progress in improving your creative intuitive abilities. For instance, you could keep a weekly rating of your performance percentage in each of the four areas of perception. You can also record the advice you get for the decisions you make and later review the results after you follow this advice or when you don't. You can write down your insights about what you believe is likely to happen in a given situation, and then compare what actually happens with your prediction to help assess your insight and make more insightful assessments in the future.

I have two books I use for keeping records. I use a new ideas book where I jot down ideas I develop with these techniques that have commercial possibilities (such as an idea for a new book, script, or game) and a daily journal where I record significant experiences and insights about what to do next in my life. I usually write down a brief synopsis of any dreams I remember and any reactions or ideas triggered by this dream, any information I feel is important after a techniques session (such as a monthly goal for activities and earnings), and significant experiences of the day (such as a meeting with someone offering a new opportunity that I must make a decision about).

Use any format that works for you, including putting your records into a file folder, recording your daily journal as a blog, or storing thoughts in a personal organizer on paper or online. Some people make a regular practice of writing down their ideas and experiences daily. While others, like me, only do this to record something that seems especially significant. Use the approach that suits you.

Generally, it is useful to keep records in these five major areas:

1) New ideas you may want to act on. This is the place to record ideas for new products, new organizational plans, new activities to try, and so forth.

2) Significant experiences of the day. This can include things like important meetings or phone calls, intuitions about people or situations, new goals you have set, accomplishments you have achieved, or predictions or plans for the future.

3) Dreams from the night before. Record as much as you can recall, along with any insights about the dream's meaning. Sometimes if you can't remember a dream immediately, meditating for a few minutes (right after waking) on any dream fragments or on awareness you had may bring the dream back. The value of writing down your dreams right after you wake is that you are more apt to remember them, and you can use your dream insights to help you better understand a current situation and make decisions. For instance, if you are thinking of taking a new job or moving to a new city and you have a dream showing the job or city in a negative light, that can be a good sign you shouldn't make the move.

4) Insights and experiences gained from using a GWYW technique. Record any experiences or ideas that stand out after a techniques session. You can record these observations during the experience, or if it's more convenient, make your record afterward.

5) Miscellaneous ideas. This might be a section at the back of your notebook where you file ideas on GWYW methods, statements to think about, illustrations, and so on.

Using GWYW Techniques to Attain Your Goals

Now you are ready to start using these techniques for specific goals. The rest of this book features exercises you can use to achieve specific objectives and gives examples of people who have used these techniques successfully.

To use this book most effectively, decide what goal you want to attain and turn to that section. Then use the exercises suggested or adapt these exercises to make them your own employing the underlying GWYW principles. For instance, if you'd rather draw a picture of what you see than write a statement about it, do so. If you'd rather get information from a wise person than a computer screen, go ahead.

The key to the effectiveness of these exercises is the principle of tapping into your creative intuition using visualization or mental imagery, and you can use any number of images and symbols to do this. The exercises described in this book are ones that have worked for others, and me, but feel free to create your own.

Chapter Two

~

Knowing When You Know

One of the most difficult things about using your intuition, either to gain insights or to make choices, is determining how you know your intuition is correct. How do you know when you are working with something as subjective as intuition? In many professions today, people use a variety of systems to make planning, setting strategies, and decision making as objective as possible. But working with intuitive and gut level sources of information and knowing those systems doesn't work.

Nevertheless, you can still get a strong sense of whether your information or choice is right by measuring your impression of the intensity of your belief and your sense of the probabilities being correct. For example, ask yourself on a scale ranging from zero to one hundred, *How strongly do I believe what I believe?* and see what employing the underlying GWYW principles number flashes into your mind. Or ask yourself on a scale of zero to one hundred, *How probable is it that the choice I am making is the right one?* and see what number comes to mind. If your response is seventy or better, you probably feel strongly that what you believe is true or that you are making the right decision. If it's ninety or above that's an even stronger indication that you feel certain about what you are doing. If you get a medium or weak response, you should reevaluate your belief or decision. You aren't really sure.

Although you are still measuring something subjective—your impression of the intensity of your belief or your sense of the probabilities—you are adding a second level of review that puts some distance between you and your initial response. It's a way of double-checking, or reconfirming, your experience.

Another way to increase your confidence in your intuition is by testing the strength of your belief or the certainty of your decision in other situations. How likely are you to be correct when you have a strong belief or sense of making the right decision? Another way to test your intuition is when you were right about something. Reflect back on how you felt when you believed something strongly or felt certain you were right.

Monitoring your feelings will help you evaluate all your intuitions because you will experience similar sensations whenever you are correct. While the system is not absolutely foolproof—it is, after all, based on subjective feelings, impressions, and beliefs—you can increase your chances for being correct or making the right choice by recognizing the signals.

Learning to Trust Your Intuitive Power

You often get feelings and premonitions that something will happen and they turn out to be correct, but other times you are wrong. The outcome isn't as you believe or suspect it will be. Someone doesn't respond as you anticipated, predicted dangers don't materialize, or an expected event doesn't happen. So how can you know when you know? How can you measure the intensity of your belief and increase your chances of correctly interpreting your intuition? For example, what would you have done in the following situation?

When Julie's landlord raised her rent she felt this was a signal to move. She had already been feeling her apartment was too small. But

where would she go? Should she stay in Santa Barbara or move to another city? She felt restless and was drawn to Los Angeles because it offered more opportunities. But should she pull up her roots?

About a week later she went on a retreat and in an exercise she saw
herself living in a house on a hill by the ocean, but it wasn't clear where
it was. She returned from the retreat more determined to move but was
still debating where to go. To help her decide, Julie drove to a residential
area near the ocean where she would want to live if she stayed in Santa Barbara. As she drove around looking for places with for rent signs,
she imagined what it would be like to live there. She saw a house two
blocks from the ocean that looked perfect. Though she couldn't see inside she felt drawn to the house, but when she called and spoke to the
real estate agent, he told her he already had an offer on the house and
wasn't taking any others. Julie felt crushed, but determined not to give
up, offered to pay a higher rent. Though the agent said he couldn't accept it, they continued to have a long conversation.

When they were done, the real estate agent commented, "It sounds
like the perfect house for you." He took her number and said maybe he
could find her something else in the area.

While Julie looked for other houses in the area, each time she drove
past this house she was drawn to it and imagined herself there. Not having any luck, she made plans to move to LA, though she still had a deep
inner feeling that she really belonged in the first house. Rationally, her
feeling made no sense. It had been more than a month since the real
estate agent had told her the house was rented. A few days before Julie
planned to spend a weekend in LA to look for a house, the agent called.
Amazingly, the house was available again because a contractor took much
longer to refurbish the house than expected and the original renters
backed out. The agent remembered their earlier conversation and now
wanted to give Julie the first chance at the house. When the agent drove
her out to look at it she immediately said yes and decided this meant she
should stay in Santa Barbara. Then after she moved in, she made other
changes in her life that helped her overcome the restlessness that led her

to consider leaving Santa Barbara and enabled her to benefit from the many established connections she already had in the area. For Julie, the experience was a lesson in listening to and trusting that deep inner sense of knowing, her feeling of being drawn to the house even after she was told it wasn't available, the correctness of the information that she gained when looking within for insights, and the image she saw when she visualized where to live.

Sometimes it's hard to recognize this knowing. Sometimes obstacles may prevent you from realizing what you know, and sometimes a positive outcome may seem impossible. Julie's experience reaffirms the importance of paying attention to your intuition and acting on it, especially when it feels so strong.

How to Know When Your Intuitions Are Correct

The key to recognizing when your intuitions are correct, and when they aren't, is to distinguish the difference in the quality and intensity of the feelings you get when your intuitions are correct and when they are not. How? By paying close attention to how you feel in both instances and noticing the differences. You can determine how your current feelings, premonitions, and beliefs compare to past patterns, and you can decide whether your intuition is correct or incorrect.

Since intuition is subjective, there are no guarantees, but this awareness of past results will increase your chances of correctly evaluating an intuitive impulse. The following exercise will help you look back and notice the differences. Review the general guidelines, or read it aloud and record it on a recording device, then play it back as you listen to the instructions.

Assessing Your Feelings and Insights

To start looking at the differences in how you feel when your intuitive impressions are correct or not you must first relax. Once you are relaxed, do the following steps.

Concentrate on your breathing for about a minute. Notice it going in and out, in and out, in and out. Now think back to a time when you had a strong feeling, premonition, or belief about something you didn't consciously know, but that later turned out to be correct. Maybe you had a feeling about what someone was really like. Maybe you had a premonition of some danger ahead. Maybe you believed something that turned out to be true. Whatever it was, focus on this incident and see it happening now. See it on the screen or area before you and watch.

Now recall the feeling you had about this event before it happened. What did it feel like? Feel that feeling now. Pay attention to how it feels.

How intense is the feeling? If you were rating it on a scale of zero to one hundred, how intense would it be? What number flashes into your mind? Where is this feeling located? In your head? Your heart or chest? Your stomach or solar plexus? All over?

Are any images or words associated with the feeling? Any pictures? Any voices? Any memories? If so, what are they like? Continue to focus on feeling that feeling. Imagine for a moment that you *are* that feeling. Now, if that feeling wanted to speak to you or give you a message, what would it say? Listen to, see, or feel that. Now let go of that feeling and that incident.

Recall another time when you had a feeling, premonition, or belief about something that turned out to be correct and follow the same steps as described in the last example.

Now think back to a time when you had a feeling, premonition, or belief about something you didn't consciously know about that later turned out to be incorrect. Maybe you thought you knew what someone was really like. Maybe you had a premonition of some danger ahead. Maybe you believed something that later turned out to be false.

Whatever it was, focus on this incident and see it happening right now. See it on the screen or area before you and watch.

Now, recall the feeling you had about this event before you discovered you were wrong. What did it feel like? Feel that feeling now. Pay attention to how it feels.

How intense is the feeling? If you were rating it on a scale of zero to one hundred, how intense would it be? What number flashes into your mind?

Where is this feeling located? In your head? Your heart or chest? Your stomach or solar plexus? All over?

Are any images or words associated with the feeling? Any pictures? Any voices? Any memories? If so, what are they like?

Is there anything about the feeling that is a signal that your intuition is not correct? Is there something about its intensity, its location, or the images or words associated with it that might be a cue to ignore this feeling? Now let go of that feeling and that incident.

Recall another time when you had a feeling, premonition, or belief about something that turned out to be wrong and again follow the steps from the previous example.

Finally, reflect on the differences you just experienced in the intensity and quality of the feelings you had when you were correct and when you were incorrect. How were they different in their intensity? Where was the feeling located? In the images or words associated with them? Those differences are cues you can use in the future to tell you whether or not to pay attention to a feeling, premonition, or belief.

Tracking Your Intuition

Another way to improve your intuitive success rate is to practice using your intuition in everyday situations, noticing the difference in the way you feel when you are correct and when you are not. Also, keep a mental or written record of how well you do. Over time you will find that your ability to know when your intuition is correct will increase.

For example, you can get immediate feedback on whether your intuitions are right or wrong by trying to determine the number of calls on your answering machine or in your voicemail when you return to your office, the number of e-mails you will receive, whether a certain person will call, whether someone will cancel an appointment, whether someone will be at a certain event, or whether someone will be a candidate or win in an election. The possibilities are endless. You can test yourself with just about anything, though in the beginning it is best to start with less important situations where you don't feel as much pressure to be right. As you test yourself, notice how certain you felt that you were correct and how accurate your impressions really were. Over time both your certainty and accuracy should go up. As you feel more certain about your ability, you can apply it to making decisions or setting expectations in situations that really matter.

Part
Two

Laying
the
Groundwork

Chapter Three

⤞

Boosting Your Energy

Another key to getting what you want is having plenty of energy so you can energetically go after what you want and exude the enthusiasm that helps you go after it. It helps to be a go-getter, and not only will that spirit help you get further toward your goal, but it will engage and motivate others to help you. It's as if by exuding that team spirit quality, you'll have a team around you supporting you and helping you to move on.

So how do you increase your energy when you want to? This chapter will focus on just how to do that and the next one is about tempering that energy so you can damp it down when you need to so you can relax. The process is like turning on a spigot of water. The hot water is full of energy that makes you active and the cold-water spigot is what cools you down so you are relaxed and calm. And you're in charge of that faucet, so you can turn on the hot water, or cold water, or mix them together whenever you want.

So for now, let's turn on that hot-water spigot so you have more energy and enthusiasm to get what you want. But a note of caution. When you think of increasing your energy, upping your mental energy is different from using energy drinks with energy enhancers or assorted

drugs that increase your energy. Certainly, many people consume assorted nutrients and drinks to increase their energy to get tasks done
more quickly, to stay awake when tired, and all sorts of other reasons,
but this is not the same as those products. You can charge your energy
using the power of your mind alone—and that's a much healthier way
to go. You draw on your own internal forces and build yourself up mentally, rather than relying on outside sources and stimulants where you
are giving over your control to the power of a drug, which can sometimes have undesirable side effects.

By contrast, when using visualization and mental imagery you are
energizing yourself naturally. You are in control of the process, including how much you want to charge yourself up, and are readily able to
mentally stop or reduce the charge as needed. So ideally, look to your
mind for a natural energy booster. In fact, recent research suggests that
changing how you think affects your brain chemistry, so your mind itself can produce its own energy-stimulating chemicals.[2] So forget drugs
and energy enhancers. You can mentally increase your energy using
only your mind.

Charging Yourself Up Mentally

Charging yourself up mentally can be invaluable, such as when you
have deadlines to meet or a seemingly impossible list of tasks to get
done in a short time.

For example, John, a freelance writer and designer, used to feel totally exhausted every few months when he had major deadlines to meet.
Suddenly, everyone had a project to be done right away and he hated to
turn any clients away because business was so unpredictable. He could
never predict when a flurry of activity would end and he would go into
a slow period. So he tried to take on everything, but the penalty was
that he often felt burned out and done in. Then, at a workshop he dis-

---

2. Margaret W. Matlin, *Cognition: 6th Edition* (New York: J. Wiley & Sons, 2005), 227.

covered that he could use mental imaging techniques to increase his energy. By visualizing the energy of the earth and air pouring into him, he was able to feel refreshed, stronger, and more powerful. As a result, he was able to revive himself by directing this energy to the task he wanted to do with the result that he could keep going and get everything done.

Similarly, there were times Maggie, who was a secretary in a large office, had dozens of things to do and didn't feel like doing them. She had been to a big party the night before, she was planning a wonderful weekend and thoughts about it kept intruding, she wasn't inspired by a particular project, or she felt miffed at a slight by her boss. Still, she knew that she had to get focused on completing these tasks and motivating herself to do it. At one time, she might have tried a few cups of coffee or a pep pill to get herself going again. But by mobilizing the powers of her mind instead, she was able to find the energy charge she needed to get to work without using anything artificial. To do so she visualized herself getting an infusion of energy from the walls of the room, imagining that the pictures that featured abstract shapes were directing powerful bursts of energy at her, like electrical charges. Then she felt that electric energy coursing through her and making her more alert and energetic. And the next day, she used the same mental charging to be bright and cheery at a big family reunion, this time imaging the energy coming to her through the entertainment center in the living room.

We all have times like these. You can undoubtedly think of many times when you want more energy to do all the things you want or need to do and need an extra energy boost to keep you going. Like John and Maggie, you need a quick energy fix to overcome feelings of fatigue, increase your creative energy, or motivate yourself to do something. While certain chemical boosters like the caffeine in those extra cups of coffee can help, too much can cause negative side effects, or even addictions. Instead, charge yourself up mentally and empower your mind naturally.

A mental charge can be especially useful when:

- You feel generally tired or sleepy during the day and can't take a nap.

- You have a series of important deadlines to meet.

- You are resisting working on a project because it feels too big or overwhelming and you need to increase your energy to get started.

- You need to be alert and enthusiastic for an activity such as going to a party, making a sales call, going to a job interview, giving a speech, giving a presentation, or leading a meeting.

- You have a difficult challenge to overcome, such as a confrontation with an in-law, boss, or employee and you need that extra shot of energy to feel up to the challenge.

- You have to come up with some ideas for a project and feel your creative energy is blocked.

- You need something to get you going in the morning and keep you going at night.

In all of these situations, and in others where you need a quick charge of energy to get moving again, you can use a variety of visualization or mental imagery techniques where you use your imagination and thoughts to create the energy you need. As a result, you don't need to use anything artificial that can upset your body chemistry and have unpleasant side effects. Instead, you are mentally drawing the energy you need from inside or from visualizing the energy coming from a source outside yourself, such as from the energy of the earth and air around you.

How These Mental Energy Boosters Work

How and why does this visualization process work to boost your energy? It does because each image or thought is a kind of electrical charge of energy that courses through your brain cells, activating neurotransmitters and other chemicals. The more focused you are in what you visualize or think, the more energy goes through your system. It's very similar to directing a hose at something. Increase the pressure enough and the water goes much farther and much faster.

Thus, anything you do to concentrate and direct your thoughts can help to raise your energy level, and because of the close mind-body connection, as your mental energy increases so will your physical energy. This relationship between mental and physical energy can be readily measured using a biofeedback device, which monitors the way the brain functions. For example, when we are at rest, asleep, or meditating our thoughts move more slowly. This is reflected in the lower frequency theta, delta, and alpha waves associated with these states. By contrast, when we are more active and alert the feedback machine registers the faster beta wave frequencies. When we dream, the increased energy of our thoughts and visual input is reflected in the faster REM waves associated with dreaming.

As a result of this brain-body relationship we can up our own energy levels by thinking high-energy thoughts, imagining stimulating images, or having strong positive feelings to make us more aware and alert. These thoughts, images, and feelings change the brain and body chemistry so we not only think we are more energetic (or feel we are), but we are also actually more physically energized.

Using Images of the Energy of the Universe to Increase Your Energy

One way to increase your energy is to draw on the energy of the universe by visualizing this energy coming into you and charging you up. The process is a little like plugging yourself into a battery charger like you might plug in a laptop or cell phone. The energy starts flowing into you, giving you a charge so you feel more energized and powerful.

To do this, imagine that you have columns of energy flowing in and through you. You can imagine the energy of the earth as more solid and grounding, the energy of the air as more light and expansive, and your own energy as a mingling of the two. Use these images to draw on the energy you feel you need most. This visualization process is particularly powerful because not only are you imagining that you are tapping into these energy sources, but you are also actually drawing this energy into you through your visualization. That's because everything in the universe is made up of molecules of energy that come together to form material objects, including you and your thoughts. At the lower theta, delta, and alpha frequencies associated with sleep and meditation our thoughts move more slowly, while at the beta frequency associated with everyday thinking we are more active and alert. In turn, the frequencies of our thoughts can influence the frequencies of our bodies. So when you use your mind powers to concentrate on raising your energy level, you are stimulating the molecules of energy in your body to move more quickly. You not only feel more energetic, but actually become more energetic. By the same token, when you focus on drawing in energy from the universe the imagery of this energy stimulates your body.

It's a technique I used when I first incorporated visualization and mental imagery techniques in my work writing regularly for clients. I would visualize myself calling on the energies of the universe to start my day so I felt ready and motivated to write. I knew I had to meet certain deadlines and I didn't want to leave anything to chance. So each morning I began the day by sitting in my living room and visualizing the energy pouring into me and swirling around through me. Then I pictured it pouring out of me into the writing assignment I had for that day. As a result I went to the typewriter (yes, we used typewriters, not computers, in those days) feeling confident I could do whatever was required, and I felt enthusiastic and motivated to get to work right away. After a few weeks I had conditioned myself to begin working every time I went to the typewriter, so I no longer needed to continue doing the exercises for this purpose. But initially this technique proved invaluable in getting me on a regular writing schedule so I could successfully complete my assignments.

Then I started using this technique in other situations, such as when I had to give a class or seminar and didn't feel in the mood, so I would feel more inspired and energetic. In this case, I would imagine the energy pouring through me and coming out through my voice. Or if I had a lot of telephone calls to make and felt reluctant to get started, I used this technique to feel the energy I needed to pick up the phone and make each call with enthusiasm. Eventually, I no longer needed to use this technique for increasing energy since the process became so automatic, but in the beginning I applied the technique again and again to feel more energized in different situations.

The power energy increasing technique can be very useful for everyone. I will explain how you can use this technique yourself. It is one of the most powerful general-purpose techniques for raising and directing energy.

Using the Energies of the Earth and Universe Technique

In this exercise you imagine the energy of the earth and the surrounding universe coursing through your body to give you the energy you need to do something you want to do. Use the following instructions as a guideline or read it aloud into a recording device and play it back as you visualize.

Start by sitting up straight with your feet on the floor and your hands facing with your palms up in a receptive position to receive this energy. Close your eyes and relax. Focus on the earth under your feet. Imagine that the earth is pulsing with energy and feel that energy flowing like a rushing river. Feel it concentrating in a radiating ball under your feet. Feel the energy rising up through the earth and surging into your feet and into your body. Notice how it rises through your feet and through your legs to the base of your spine. Feel it warming and charging you as it rises. Feel it expand out through your torso, into your arms, and head. Feel it giving you its strength and power as it spreads through you.

As this energy continues to pour into you, notice that the energy of the universe or atmosphere around you is focusing into a ball of bright, radiant, pulsing energy at the top of your head. Now experience this energy coming in through the top of your head. You can see and feel it pouring in and you feel it energizing you as it does. Notice that this energy feels light, airy, and expansive.

Next, experience this energy traveling through your head into your spine, into your arms, and spiraling down your torso. It feels light, airy, and expansive as it radiates through your body.

Now, focus on the two energies meeting at the base of your spine, fusing together to charge you up even more by their combined powers. The energy of the earth is charging you with its strength and power, and the energy of the universe is charging you with the feeling of light-ness and expansion. Notice how the two energies merge, blend, and spi-ral together like a big, bright, pulsing ball of energy. Experience them moving up and down your spine, radiating throughout your body, fill-ing you with energy. You can balance the two energies, if you wish, by drawing on extra energy from the earth for more strength and power or from the air for more lightness and expansion. Keep this energy run-ning up and down your spine and throughout your body until you feel filled and charged with energy.

Next, direct this energy toward whatever project or task you want to do. You will feel very motivated and excited to do it, even if you didn't feel motivated before, were resisting, or felt afraid to start this project. How you felt in the past no longer matters because you are now full of energy. You have the energy and enthusiasm to tackle the project and you feel confident you can do it. Even if you felt blocked before, you feel your creative juices flowing within you now and you know you are able and ready to perform this task. As you direct this energy, see it flowing out of you as needed so you can do this project. Whatever you are going to do, see the energy coursing through you as needed so you can direct it to that purpose.

For example, if you want to write or type something, visualize the energy surging out through your hands. If you are going to give a speech or presentation, see the energy surging into your throat and charging up whatever you are going to say. If you are going to lift heavy objects, visualize the energy coming out through your feet, body, and hands, giving you extra strength. Whatever you need to do, see the energy coursing through you as needed so you can do whatever you want.

Finally, return to the room and open your eyes, feeling charged with this energy. Once you have finished this exercise, plunge immediately into your project. You'll suddenly have lots of energy and enthusiasm.

Other Mental Energy Boosting Exercises

While the energy of the universe is great for charging you up to do a particular task or project, other exercises are alternate ways of using mental imagery and focusing your mind to increase your mental, emotional, and physical energy level. The first exercise involves giving yourself both a physical and mental energy jolt, which is a great wake-up for whatever you are doing. The second exercise involves drawing on the energy from your experience of past situations where you have felt high-energy. The third involves imagining you have more energy in the situation you are in. Use the approach that works best for you, or if you like, use a combination of these techniques to raise your energy.

Creating Your Own Energy and Enthusiasm

This technique works as a great energy pick-me-up, like giving yourself a shot of mental caffeine to get you going for whatever you are doing. Stand with your feet slightly apart and make a fist with one hand. Then, quickly raise your hand to your head and lower it several times. Each time you bring it down, shout out something like any of the following phrases:

- I am awake.

- I feel energetic.

- I am enthusiastic and excited.

- I am raring to get up and go.

Repeat this five to ten times. As you do this feel a rush of energy and enthusiasm surge through you, and soon you'll be awake, alert, and ready to tackle any project. If other people are around so you can't actively participate in this exercise, imagine yourself doing it in your mind's eye. It's more stimulating to use your whole body, but using your mind powers alone will help wake you up or motivate you to act.

For instance, I've used it at seminars and conferences to wake myself up when I felt I was drifting off. I'd simply concentrate on being awake and alert in my mind's eye and repeat a key phrase such as what is listed above again and again in my mind. Then, in a few minutes I would typically feel ready to go or listen again.

Drawing on Past Energy

In this exercise you imagine a situation in your past where you experienced a high level of energy. Then you imagine yourself having this same energy to deal with a current situation. Get relaxed in a quiet place. Focus on your breathing going in and out until you have calmed down and feel completely relaxed.

Now imagine yourself traveling back in the past to a time when you were especially energetic. Just see yourself going back as you take an elevator or train back in time. When you arrive, step into a situation where you felt especially active and full of energy. Maybe it was a social occasion, an event you attended, or somewhere special you went. Whatever it is, see yourself there now and experience that sense of high energy and excitement.

Take a few minutes and feel the strength and power of that high energy and excitement. You feel very excited, very alert, very charged up.

Now, keeping that feeling of high energy in mind, come back into the room. You can take that energy and use it. You will feel full of energy, excited, very alert, and ready to do whatever you need to do.

Imagining High Energy

In this exercise you focus on increasing your level of energy in the present situation, either just before doing something or by taking a break during the experience to recharge your energy batteries.

Find a quiet place to get relaxed or tune out whatever is going on around you if you can. Then focus on your breathing going in and out until you have calmed down and feel completely relaxed.

Now, picture the situation you are about to enter or what you have just taken a break from. Imagine yourself having great confidence and resolve. You feel you know exactly what to say and exactly what to do. You feel very good and very sure of yourself.

Take a moment to notice whatever it is you are going to do. Imagine yourself interacting with others like you are in a scene from a movie. As you visualize this scene, notice you are feeling more and more energetic and more and more enthusiastic. Your feeling of ease as you relate to others or engage in this activity helps you feel very focused and very alert. You feel charged up, excited, and raring to go.

Now take a few moments to feel that energy, alertness, and enthusiasm rising up in you. Feel it spreading through you. It is radiating out through your arms, your legs, your torso, and your head. You feel as if you're radiating and glowing with energy.

Keeping that feeling of high energy in mind, come back into the room. You can go right into the situation taking that high energy with you. You feel full of energy, excited, alert, and ready to plunge in and do whatever you have to do.

Don't Forget to Sleep

While these energy-raising techniques are designed to increase your energy and can give you an added boost when you feel tired so you can do more, they are not designed to replace needed sleep. Occasionally when you miss some sleep, like when you are on a deadline crunch or have an especially full schedule, an energy-raising technique can fill the bill. But the key word here is *occasionally*. These techniques are not meant to replace getting enough sleep on a regular basis. If you find you are frequently tired or often drift off while doing something, you obviously need more sleep and should get it. On a short-term basis, these techniques are ideal for increasing your energy when you need it for a particular project or event or giving yourself a quick energy fix.

Chapter Four

∽

Overcoming Stress

Achieving a Balance Between Stress and Relaxation to Get What You Want

It goes without saying that if you feel overly stressed, anxious, or tense, that'll interfere with getting what you want. Not only can these things interfere with your health (think high blood pressure, heart attacks, and other problems linked to these reactions), but you are also more likely to make mistakes, errors of judgment, bad decisions, and otherwise screw up whatever you are doing. Just think of all the accidents from car accidents to airplane mishaps to ship oil spills, and you have the idea. From driver to pilot to controller error, being overstressed and anxious can definitely screw you up. You could end up ill, injured, attacked, in trouble, or even dead, and much further away from ever achieving your goal.

Unfortunately, stress is very common in the workplace, at home, and in life today and these tensions can carry over into other aspects of life. A key reason for this heightened stress is the pressure of our competitive and success-oriented age. There are pressures to perform, to meet deadlines, to do well, to be better than the competition, to get a contract, to obtain a job, to be promoted, to look successful, to make your family proud … and so on. They come with the territory of trying to accomplish things and succeed.

On the other hand, a little stress can be stimulating and encourage people to do better. For example, when a speaker feels a twinge of anxiety before giving a talk, they usually do well because that small amount of stress triggers extra adrenalin so the speaker has more energy and is primed for performing. Or a bride at a wedding can really shine because of that extra adrenalin pumped up by all the stress that goes into planning and meeting and greeting dozens of guests.

But when the stress level gets too high it interferes with performance and may even make performance impossible. Instead of pushing the person to peak performance, the extra energy becomes unmanageable and turns into a serious case of nerves. A performance may be blocked.

By the same token, when a person worries about meeting a deadline it can stimulate them to work harder and faster to accomplish what needs to be done. But with too many worries, a person can get caught up in a vicious cycle in which these negative thoughts become the focus of attention and shut out productive thoughts that contribute to the goal. Thus, learning to relax and getting rid of unwanted tension becomes critical for working effectively and having a satisfying, successful life. The key is to watch for signs that one is overly tense or overstressed. Then work on creating an appropriate balance between the slight tensions needed to stimulate an effective performance and the need to be sufficiently relaxed to feel confident, composed, and carry out any task smoothly and efficiently.

In turn, these GWYW techniques can help you apply the relaxation or stress reduction techniques that work for you. These work in tandem with the energy-increasing techniques described in the last chapter. Use those energy enhancers when you need more energy and enthusiasm to drive you to achieve what you want. Use the stress reducers to relax and calm down as a counterbalance to feeling revved up, anxious, tense, or stressed out.

How GWYW Techniques Can Help

The following example illustrates how well the GWYW techniques can help you relax and get rid of unwanted stress. It shows how a hard-driving executive was able to do it, and if someone in a high stress occupation can do it, anyone can.

Dave was a typical Type A executive. Head of marketing and sales for a small communications manufacturing company, he was always rushing from one appointment to another. He was always determined to do everything he could to close whatever deal he was working on at the time. He drove the salespeople he supervised hard, and when someone didn't make a sale he grilled the person in excruciating detail about what went wrong, making the person feel more like a defendant facing a judge. Likewise, when he failed to make a sale himself or didn't sell as much as he expected, he mentally chastised himself. Not surprisingly, he not only experienced a high level of turnover in his sales force, but he also often felt like a bundle of nerves when he went out on a sales call. His doctor even warned him he would be a good candidate for an ulcer if he kept going on this way.

Instead, Dave needed to learn how to relax and let go of the day-to-day pressures he felt, which manifested out of his intense fear of failure. His first step in letting go was becoming aware of when he felt particularly anxious and reminding himself to release that tension. To do so he sought to conclude whatever he was doing as quickly as possible and spend some time alone in his office calming himself down. If he was on the road, Dave would park his car in a quiet spot, turn off the radio, and concentrate on quieting his mind.

Using a calming exercise such as described in chapter 1, he then focused on calming down. He took a few minutes to pay attention to his breathing, tightened and released his muscles, or saw himself getting more relaxed as he went down in an elevator. After a few minutes, these relaxation exercises took effect and he felt his tension dissipate. To prevent the anxiety from returning once he went back to work, he asked his inner mind what he needed to do to stay relaxed. He remained in his relaxed, meditative state of mind to ask, *Why am I so tense right now?* Then he asked, *What do I need to do to stay calm?*

After he asked each question, he listened for the answer. The response to the first question came quickly: "You must let go of feeling you *need* to make the sale. You must listen to the customer and then do your best. But do not blame yourself or your salespeople for not succeeding. Just do your best and tell them to do the same. You can't expect to achieve 100 percent all the time."

In answer to his second question, the voice in his mind said, "Keep reminding yourself what you must do. Tell yourself you must let go and stop blaming yourself. Tell yourself you must do your best and that's all you can expect. When you feel tense, tell yourself, *I'm relaxed. I'm letting go. I'm doing the best I can. I am relaxed.* Keep saying this to yourself for as long as you need to. Then, you'll calm down and be fine."

Once he got these answers Dave returned to work repeating these messages to himself, determined to let go, listen, and do his best without feeling he had to succeed. At first he struggled to keep away the usual thoughts about accomplishment that contributed to his anxieties. But gradually, as he repeated these exercises, he found the periods of relaxation and reduced tension lasted longer and longer, until finally even the people around him noticed the change. His salespeople found his disposition sunnier and they felt motivated to work harder. They also performed better as he eased his demands on them. He found his own sales negotiations with customers improved. He was less intense and driven with them so they could feel more relaxed working with him. In turn, as he listened to his customers more and learned more about what they wanted, he was better able to create win-win solutions. The result was more sales and a higher average volume for each one. Dave felt even more confident and relaxed. In time, he no longer needed to use these exercises because the problem had been resolved. However, the GWYW techniques had triggered the initial relaxation and tension reduction that led to his ultimate success.

How to Overcome Stress and Tension

Dave's story illustrates the basic steps to reducing and eliminating unwanted stress and tension so you can be better primed to get what you want. The basic steps are to calm down using a relaxation technique, understand the source of your stress or tension, decide what you need to do to get rid of this source of tension, and chase away any worries about the problem. Use the following steps to implement this process to help you overcome stress.

Calm Down with a Relaxation Technique

You can use any of the techniques described in chapter 1 for this. In addition, develop a trigger for yourself so whenever you feel stress coming on, you can catch yourself and remain calm and relaxed. To create this trigger, end your relaxation exercise with a suggestion that whenever you want to relax, you can bring together the thumb and middle finger of your right hand and repeat to yourself several times, *I am calm. I am relaxed.* Or create your own triggering device that suggests relaxation to you. During the day whenever you feel under pressure use your trigger to help calm down. Or you can do even more, as will be discussed in later chapters. Suppose you feel stressed because you are going to meet your mother-in-law who is usually very critical. On the way, use your trigger to calm yourself down and again reinforce that message by reminding yourself that you feel calm and relaxed. You might even use the image of a duck with any feelings of tension washing away from the duck's feathers into the cooling waters of a pond.

The advantage of this relaxation approach is that it helps calm you down and relieves mild symptoms of stress. However, it doesn't deal with the underlying reasons why you are feeling stressed. So for a deeper, more

permanent solution, take additional steps to understand what you are doing to make yourself tense and learn how you can get rid of this source of
tension by coming up with alternative actions.

The Source of Your Stress and Tension

To find out the reason you feel tense, get in a relaxed frame of mind
and mentally ask yourself why you are so tense, like Dave did. Then
listen to whatever thoughts or images immediately pop into your mind.
You will find that encouraging this spontaneity will give you insights
into your inner feelings and concerns. If you have any difficulty getting
a full response to your questions there are two things you can do to spur
your inner processes. You can either imagine that you are talking to an
inner guide or counselor, or that you are getting the information you
seek on a computer console or movie screen. Write down any thoughts
or images on a sheet of paper using automatic writing to make your
thoughts flow more freely.

How to Get Rid of the Source

Once you have determined the reason for your stress, the next step is
asking yourself what you should do about it. When you ask the question about what is making you so tense, put yourself in a receptive
frame of mind so you can get the answer from your intuition or inner
self, which will have the answers for you on what to do. Now it's time
to ask the second question of what you need to do to stay calm. Again,
don't try to shape your answer consciously, but be receptive to what
your inner mind tells you. For more information, ask yourself, *What else
must I do to stay calm?*

As before, the key to communicating with your inner powers is encouraging your inner spontaneity to tell you the information you need
to know. Once again, use an inner guide, counselor, screen, or automatic writing to encourage the process if you encounter any resistance to

your question. You can use whatever form works best for you. The key is to make it as accessible for you as possible.

Chase Away Any Worries about the Problem

The final step is to chase away any worries and fears about achieving the results you want. These worries are like an internal negative dialogue we have with ourselves where we state everything we can't do that prevents us from doing something, or we assert our fears about why what we want won't occur. But such concerns are totally unproductive and do nothing but increase our feelings of stress.

For instance, take that important strategy meeting described earlier. You may already feel anxious and tense because you consider it crucial to make a good impression, but these worries take away your inner confidence that you can do it. Instead, they get you concerned that maybe you can't, that you won't be good enough, or that the other people in the meeting may not understand.

Or suppose you are worried about a conversation with your significant other where you want to make some changes in responsibilities around the house. If you get stuck in worrying about how things might go wrong, you might be too afraid to say anything at all, so nothing will change. Or you may become so emotional when you discuss the subject that instead of a constructive process of working together to make changes, you may end up in a screaming battle that makes the problem even worse.

Your worries lead you to churn the situation over and over in your mind because you're afraid of how the event will turn out and fear the worst. The result is that your worries make you feel terrible and your negative thoughts contribute to the very outcome you fear. If you're worried you won't give a good presentation, you probably won't. You'll lack the confidence you need and your whole manner will convey the impression that you don't think you are any good. Furthermore, your worries can interfere with implementing the answers you get about methods to relieve stress just as they can lead you to think these techniques won't work. Thus, if you've got any worries or fears standing in the way of overcoming your feelings of tension, you've got to eliminate them. You can do so in four ways:

- Come up with one or more alternatives to deal with the current situation so you can take some action to make changes in the way things are now. Select the alternative you like the most.
- Visualize the outcome you want and your focus on this outcome will help bring about the desired result.
- Remind yourself that you will do it to build confidence.
- Affirm that whatever happens is what should happen, so you can accept what comes and feel satisfied with it.

Depending on the situation, you can use one or a combination of these techniques. When you are done, turn your thoughts to something else unless you have planned to take a specific action, so the inner powers released by your concentration can work within you to help create the change you want. The process is like eliminating the underbrush that is standing in the way of your walking or riding along a path, or getting rid of walls or fences barring your way. To get where you are going quickly and effectively, you've got to have a clear path ahead. Read further to find ways of putting these four methods into action to get what you want.

Come Up with an Alternative

In this technique, imagine that your inner voice is speaking to you in the form of a series of scenes in a movie and you are the director. As you imagine the scene, let the characters come up with events that suggest alternatives you might use to help you attain your objective.

Start by seeing yourself as the director on a film set. You sit in your director's chair, which is in the same location that you are having your current problem. You are also holding a script that is about this problem. The actors are waiting in the wings for their cue to start playing it out and one of the characters represents you. As you watch for a few moments, the characters act out the events leading up to the present situation. If this is a work problem, the actors will be your boss, work associates, or employees. If you have a family disagreement, imagine yourself talking to other family members. The characters play the scene just as you have remembered it.

As the action comes to the present time, ask yourself, *What does the script say I should do now?* Then listen to the reply. Your inner voice may have several suggestions that you can try, or it may tell you to wait and relax. If your inner voice is uncertain it means that you should not actively do anything right now to affect the situation. Even if you do not make any movements on the situation, you can still visualize the outcome you want, or affirm your willingness to accept whatever the outcome will be. Whatever the result, feel you can trust your inner voice so there is no need to worry any longer. Then act, wait, or relax as suggested and feel confident that the appropriate outcome will occur.

Visualize the Desired Outcome

If you already know the outcome you would like, visualize that occurring to make those results more likely. For example, if you want your coworkers to go along with your suggestions at a meeting, see yourself presenting a forceful argument and see them agreeing with what you say. Meanwhile, as you see this outcome, feel confident it will happen so you can put any worries about the results out of your mind. Whatever the situation is, you can script it in advance and then visualize what you want to happen, which will reinforce your desired goal.

Here's an example of how you might imagine a better outcome to a current situation. See yourself in a private office at work or at home in your living room. Even if you don't currently have a private office or living room, imagine that you do and it is very comfortable and quiet. Now, imagine it is the present and you are thinking about the situation that has been bothering you.

Suddenly, there is a knock on the door. You get up, answer it, and a messenger hands you an envelope that says URGENT in big red letters. You open the envelope, read the letter, and feel ecstatic because the letter informs you that everything is the way you would like it to be. For the next few minutes concentrate on seeing the desired situation before you. You have exactly what you want.

Remind Yourself You Will Do It

You can also chase away your fears about a task by building up your confidence about doing it. A simple way to do this is to remind yourself during the day that you can and will do whatever you plan to do. Take a few quiet minutes to get calm and centered, and repeat the following mantra to yourself several times with intense concentration, filling in the first blank with an image of what you want to do and filling in the second sentence with an image of actually doing it.

I can do _____. I am doing _____.

The key is to see yourself doing whatever you hope to do *now* so your inner mind gets used to you doing it. Also, feel a sense of assurance and confidence that you are doing this activity correctly and effectively. Perhaps visualize others being pleased and complimenting you on something you have done, such as writing a good report, giving a good presentation, leading a successful meeting, or persuading your partner to take a vacation where you want to go. You'll feel better immediately. You'll be calmer, more relaxed, and less worried about what you have to do. In addition, when it comes time to perform the activity, you'll do it better because you feel more confident and have already rehearsed it in your mind.

Affirm Your Acceptance

No matter how much you try to actively or mentally influence events, circumstances sometimes may not turn out as you hoped. Yet, in the long run, things often will turn out for the best if you are only patient. Jane was a project supervisor in an ad agency and felt very depressed for several days when she didn't get a research project assignment after she wrote up a twenty-page proposal for it. But a few weeks later she learned about an even bigger project, and using the information she had put together for her original proposal she was able to turn out an excellent response to the project administrators in record time. They were impressed and she got the job.

One important key to overcoming worries is to realize that often things may seem to go wrong, but you can turn them around or use what happened as a learning experience to create something even better. Another way to think of initially undesirable events is to realize that your wants and needs often differ, and when they do, you usually get what you need.

For example, a person longs for a new job title with additional responsibilities and a new office, but they don't have sufficient experience to handle the job and would be over their head, and perhaps fired, if promoted right away. Or a person is heartbroken when the person they plan to marry decides to marry someone else, but someone else turns out to be the perfect partner. It is important to develop a feeling of acceptance about whatever happens as well as trying to do your best to achieve your goals. If you feel you have done everything possible to attain a goal but don't get it, calmly accept the outcome. It is important that you have done your all, and now it's time to be receptive and patient until the next opportunity presents itself.

The value of this approach is that you align yourself with the flow of events rather than fighting against the current. Further, you are basing your actions on the premise that nothing in the universe happens by coincidence, but rather the universe seems to respond to our needs by providing exactly what we require. Thus, what happens is what should. In turn, if you use this premise to guide your life, you will find everything much easier for you. You'll still try as hard as you can to attain your goals, but you'll also feel a sense of satisfaction and completion regardless of what happens, knowing that somehow you can profit from the experience and consider it to be for the best in the long run. The following visualization will help you develop this power of acceptance.

See yourself seated in a park near where you live or work. The sun is shining brightly and it is very quiet and peaceful. You are enjoying a lunch break and you feel calm, relaxed, and receptive to whatever comes.

Now, from the distance some people arrive carrying small wrapped packages tied with ribbons. These people look like they might have come from one of the stores in your neighborhood, and they come to you and hand you the packages as a gift.

As you open each package you find a different present inside. It may be money, an object, or a certificate providing some service to you. Some gifts you want, others you need, and others are unexpected. But as you open each gift, you receive them with equal acceptance and you calmly say to the person who gave it to you, "Thank you, I accept." Then that person leaves and you receive and open the next package. You continue receiving these gifts until all of the gift bearers have finished giving their gifts to you.

As you get up to leave, remind yourself that these gifts represent the experiences and challenges you encounter in life. And just as you have received and accepted each gift, you must receive and accept each experience that comes. You must participate to the best of your ability and use the experience to learn and grow, but whatever it is, you must learn to accept it. This is the secret of staying calm and relaxed, overcoming stress, and getting rid of worries. You must learn to receive and accept, as well as to achieve and grow.

Chapter Five

☙

Controlling Your Emotions

Sometimes you will find barriers to getting what you want because of your negative emotions, such as angers and fears. You can use the GWYW techniques to deal with these emotions, too, and get them out of the way just as you can use these techniques to overcome bad habits.

First let's deal with the emotions. Your positive emotions such as love and joy are great motivators in stimulating you to get what you want because you enjoy the results and feel more creative and productive. Your negative emotions such as anger and fear can also provide a benefit at times by protecting and defending you. They can warn you about things that might hurt you or they can mobilize you to strike back at something harmful. For example, the flight or fight response triggered by danger is a survival mechanism, as applicable to the corporate jungle as the real jungle and to problems in personal relationships. Instead of fighting a hostile lion with a weapon or running away, you fight a corporate or personal adversary to win in a power struggle, or go along or retreat if you can't.

At other times, however, these negative emotions can stand in the way of achieving your goals. Such as when you have unreasonable fears and anxieties or when you lose control of your emotions. If you don't control your anger or frustration, you can blow something small into a big insult that turns into a feud. And that will not only make you feel worse but can also result in you losing a job or not getting a desired promotion. Even when an uncontrolled explosion seems to achieve its immediate purpose, it can still have long-term negative effects on relationships and on personal satisfaction. By contrast, if you stay in charge of your emotions or turn anger into a diplomatic or creative way of asking for or going after what you want, you can avoid problems and achieve your goals.

How Uncontrolled Emotions Can Stand in Your Way

You can probably think of numerous examples when giving in to uncontrolled emotions can lead to exactly what you don't want. That's what happened to Mary who was in a custody battle with her ex-husband, Duncan, over their teenage son. Duncan was offering to share joint custody, but she was so angry with him because he had broken up with her after several years due to her growing involvement in local political groups and his career requiring extensive travel. When he was finally promoted to a position where he would be home more, the emotional distance between them had grown too much. While she agreed divorce was for the best so they could each get on with their lives, her discovery that he was seeing and planning to a marry another woman made her burn with rage. So even though Duncan would be living an hour away in an upscale suburb, she didn't want him to see their child. It was her only way to punish him. And the thought of another woman stepping into the picture as the stepmother made her feel even angrier and determined to keep him and their son apart.

Her insistence led to a screaming fight on the phone, which ended with her saying, "Talk to my lawyer." This was followed by fights with her lawyer who urged her to work out a joint custody agreement with Duncan since he was in a position to provide their child with a good home. This approach made sense, but her anger made her refuse and led to a series of family court hearings. This only increased the legal bills and resulted in a judge ruling for joint custody and spelling out a formal agreement of who had the child when. Meanwhile, her son saw the raging battle and turned against her for being unreasonable and was uncommunicative with her. In the end her anger led her to undermine the relationship with her son that she wanted as well as running up costly legal expenses that led to the joint custody result anyway.

For a moment her expression of anger had made her feel better since she initially put a barrier in the way of Duncan seeing their son, but the results were self-destructive both for herself and for her child. Had Mary been able to control her emotions and been willing to discuss alternatives rationally, she may have been able to work out an amicable arrangement that would have preserved a better relationship with her child and saved time, money, and stress.

How could she have achieved that result? By taking some time out to calm down, using some calming self-talk, or using a physical trigger to remind herself that she was getting irrationally angry and needed to do something to calm down.

Controlling the Expression of Emotions to Get What You Want

While the uncontrolled expression of emotion can be self-destructive like in Mary's case, the controlled expression of emotion can be just what you need to achieve the desired effect if used at the right time. The following techniques can help you channel and control your emotions so you express them in creative ways or avoid expressing them in ways that will be destructive to yourself and others. This way you can express your emotions or hold them back as appropriate to the situation.

Since anger is the most destructive of the negative emotions, we will focus first on how to control and channel your anger as well as any feelings that can trigger it, such as jealousy, envy, resentment, or feelings of betrayal. You can apply these techniques to controlling and channeling other negative emotions, too.

Recognize Your Feelings

The first step toward getting your feelings under control and channeling them is to become aware of how you feel. Then you can acknowledge these feelings and stop yourself from expressing them in an inappropriate way or at an inopportune time. It is clear that you are angry if you yell or scream, tell someone off, or otherwise demonstrate anger. But even before these outward expressions there are mental or physical signs of anger. If you are aware of them before you explode, you can short-circuit the process and mentally decide if you want to express your anger or not. In fact, domestic violence support groups that try to help one partner overcome their violence against the other partner use such an approach. They help the abuser become aware of the signs of their anger so they can hold themselves back and channel it away from abusing their partner. You can use the following exercise to help you recognize the signs of anger before you express them in destructive ways.

Picking Up on the Signs of Anger

Get in a calm, relaxed frame of mind. Focusing on the screen in your mind's eye, think back to a time when you were angry. See the scene appear before you like a film. Then imagine you are winding the film back to a time before the incident occurred that provoked your anger. Watch the scene unfold.

Now pay attention to how you experienced this. Be aware of the sensations in your body and of how you are holding yourself. Notice any changes in your muscle tension. Notice any changes in your self-talk or the thoughts going on in your mind. Notice how you are feeling when you are angry or are becoming angry.

Then let go of that image. Turn the projector off or rewind the film. Feel yourself releasing any anger and experience that release. Then notice the differences in how you feel now and how you felt before. Be aware of the way you felt when you were angry or becoming angry compared to when you are not. Now repeat the process to see if there are other ways you experience becoming or being angry, or to become more aware of the way you felt by using a different anger scenario than the first example.

You are now very comfortable, very calm, and very peaceful, although you are conscious of how you react when you are angry and know you may react that way in the future. These are the signs to look for when you feel yourself becoming angry in the future. Then, keeping these signs in mind, but feeling very comfortable, calm, and peaceful, let go of what you have experienced and return to the room.

Five Ways to Control Your Anger

Once you feel the signs of anger coming on, you can stop yourself from expressing it or channel it to avoid expressing it inappropriately or destructively, if you wish. The goal is to manage the expression of your feelings so you express them wisely. Following are five effective ways to stop, deflect, channel, or otherwise control your feelings of anger:

1) Ask for, or take, a time out. This is a way to get away from the situation or person who is causing you to feel angry. This time out also gives you a chance to calm down, get your feelings under control, and check assumptions or information that is causing you to feel angry. After all, you could be wrong. Time outs can be combined with one of the visualization techniques discussed later that can help you let go of and release or redirect your anger in a more positive way.

2) Use calming self-talk. By telling yourself calming things you direct your attention away from what is bothering you and

counter the physical feelings that are contributing to your anger. Calming self-talk can also short-circuit any immediate impulse you have to lash out verbally or physically and help you feel more detached and less emotional about the situation. You may tell yourself things like, *Calm down. Relax. This problem isn't so important. You don't have to react now. Don't take this personally. Don't let this bother you.* You can also use self-talk to guide you into personal projection or detachment.

3) Use personal projection to remove yourself from the situation. In this case you imagine you are not there. You mentally go away or experience yourself stepping out of yourself and watching so you are no longer emotionally affected by the situation you are in. Although you are fully aware of and in charge of the process, you become like an observer or film director rather than an actor in your own film. You can use self-talk to guide you into this state, or simply visualize or experience yourself somewhere else.

4) Don't take it personally. This is a good way to deflect the tendency to react defensively when someone's negative or accusatory behavior is less due to something you have done than triggered by their own problems. If you can tell yourself, *It isn't me ... he/she is just angry and is taking it out on me,* you can distance yourself from the situation so you feel less upset and angry. Then you may find that if you just listen and don't express your anger the other person will share what is really going on and the problem will resolve itself.

5) Let go of your anger through visualization. While some visualizations can be done quickly (even in the midst of the situation causing you anger), others take longer and generally require some private time. So this visualization technique is best when you apply it to an ongoing situation or you are able to take some time out.

Explained below are some examples of visualizations that can assist you to let go of any anger. Choose those that feel most comfortable to you, combine two or more visualizations, or create your own.

Five Visualizations for Releasing Anger

Grounding It Out

As you feel the anger rising within you, visualize it coming in like a beam of negative energy from the person or situation that is upsetting you. Then imagine this energy moving down within you and dispersing harmlessly into the ground.

Blocking Out the Cause

Imagine a bubble, dome, or wall of white light of protection around you. This object is a barrier between you and the situation or person causing the anger. As you sit or stand behind this barrier you can deflect everything the person says or the events that produce anger. You are safe, isolated, and protected inside.

Projecting It Out and Eliminating It

Get in a very relaxed state and imagine a large screen in front of you. Then, imagine you are projecting the anger within you like a laser beam onto the screen. Next, imagine you are holding a raygun and shooting at that anger. Each time you zap it you experience the anger releasing and draining away.

Making the Person Causing the Anger Smaller

This method is especially suitable if the person causing the anger has a strong emotional hold over you. To release your anger, make that person seem smaller, less powerful, and less important to you. Start by seeing yourself talking to this person. See them doing whatever makes you angry. Then, as you talk, see this person shrink in size. Notice their voice becoming fainter and fainter. Meanwhile, you feel stronger and more powerful while this person becomes less powerful and important in your life. Then see yourself saying goodbye and leaving this tiny person while you feel very powerful. Finally, let go of this image and return to your everyday consciousness.

Taking Mental Revenge

While this method can be a helpful release for some people, others may find it makes them angrier. Use it if you find it's a helpful catharsis, but if you feel your anger level going up, don't continue with this method. To use this technique, get into a relaxed state and imagine taking some action to appropriately punish the person who has wronged you. In the beginning, ask yourself, *What can I do to get a just punishment or revenge for* _____? Fill in the blank with a description of what the person has done. Then, like in a film, just sit back and observe what happens and let yourself enjoy it.

Afterward, let go of the experience and return to normal consciousness. When you do, notice if you feel better. If so, this is a good technique for you. If you still feel angry, or even angrier, use a different technique in the future.

Learn from the Experience to Release Your Anger

Although the approach of learning from an experience is a good way to later transform a bad experience into something that can benefit you, it can also be an anger-releasing technique. It helps release anger because knowing that the situation can later be used for your own benefit can help you feel better as it happens. This awareness can help you detach and see the situation in a more neutral way because you realize that you have the ability to transform what is negative into something positive. To use this technique, create a reminder to yourself to help you feel better. It can be something like telling yourself, *I'll be able to learn from or profit from this experience later, so don't be so upset now.*

If possible at the time, think, *What can I learn from this situation that I can use in the future?* Or *How can I turn this situation into something from which I can profit?* If you can't ask these questions at the time the event is happening, ask them later in a quiet or private place. Consider how the bad experience you have just had can be used to teach you something, guide you in the future, or be turned into a stepping-stone to an opportunity that you gain something from. By reminding yourself that every experience has a positive potential and knowing that you can take some time later to realize these positive possibilities, you can help release your emotional upset and anger.

Chapter Six

✐

Getting Rid
of Negative Thinking

Just as negative emotions can be a barrier to getting what you want, so can negative thinking, such as when your inner critical judge puts you down with thoughts of, *I'm not good enough to get it.* Such thinking can undermine your confidence and cause you to unconsciously sabotage your goal, whatever that may be. In the end your actions prove your thinking.

Likewise, having a negative view of the world where you expect the worst to happen, fear any change, and think things will only get worse will only help to guarantee that things will go wrong. Then when they do it reinforces the "I told you so" attitude. Your negative outlook guides the way you act, which in turn contributes to you not getting what you want. While it can be great to focus on having a positive attitude and convincing yourself that you are on your way to getting what you want, if you have any feelings of ambivalence about whether you can do it or whether that's really what you want, you can be undermining your own efforts to achieve your objectives. Having negative thoughts about yourself can likewise undermine your confidence and ability to get what you want.

So, if any such negative thoughts or attitudes are holding you back, don't let them. Just as habits can be broken, blocks to your success can also be eliminated.

Turning Negative Into Positive Thinking for Success

Since negative thinking feeds upon itself, it can be difficult to break the cycle. In fact, many people with a negative outlook feel more comfortable when an obstacle turns up because that not only reinforces their usual attitude, but they can also use the obstacle as an excuse for not achieving their desired goal. Sadly, many people learn to enjoy complaining as a way to gain satisfaction from all the things that go wrong. It's the "misery loves company" phenomenon—unhappy people look for someone to complain to and then feel better for the support and sharing. When complaining becomes a way of life, the cycle is difficult to break. Complainers don't realize that their attitude contributes to the many misadventures they experience. Indeed, research shows that a negative attitude can contribute to illness and slow down the healing process, while a positive attitude contributes to wellness and healing. Our attitudes and emotions actually change the chemistry in our brain to make us function more or less effectively.[3]

Luckily, negative attitudes and thinking can be changed. We can actively intervene to break and change a cycle of negative feelings and experiences—with dramatic positive results. That's what happened to Madeline. As the youngest child, she had two older brothers who constantly criticized her and she came to think of herself as always being wrong. By extension, she came to view everything around her that way as well. If something hadn't yet gone wrong in her life, she thought it probably would. She looked for faults in other people and in the world

---

3. Bill D. Moyers, *Healing and the Mind* (New York: Doubleday, 1993).

in general. It helped her feel better about herself. Because she was so judgmental and negative she had few friends, and because she found things wrong with others she liked few people, and people, in turn, didn't like her. She complained of being lonely, never realizing it was she who pushed people away. At the same time, she wondered why her life seemed to go so badly. She worried about what would happen next, believing it would go wrong. She often nixed suggestions for the future, fearing what might happen. Thus, her negativity created blocks in her relationships and cut her off from many opportunities.

But even Madeline was able to change after decades of negative thinking by using assorted techniques to become aware of when she was being negative, stop the chain of negative thinking, and replace these thoughts with positive, motivating ones. Similarly, you can make such changes through awareness, putting the brakes on negativity, and embracing the positive.

Getting Rid of Negative Thoughts and Attitudes by Reprogramming Yourself

If, like Madeline, you have negative attitudes and patterns that interfere with getting what you want in any area of your life, you can change these attitudes and thoughts with positive personal reprogramming. This technique helps turn negative attitudes and patterns into positive ones. It involves becoming aware of your negative and pessimistic thinking and reminding yourself again and again to shift your orientation. Eventually this new outlook becomes a new positive habit. The basic process is a simple one, though it involves repeated concentration to reinforce the desired change until it becomes automatic. The following techniques illustrate ways you can stop your negative thinking and turn the negatives into positives. While I've incorporated symbols and suggestions that have worked for me, what's important are the principles underlying these techniques. Feel free to adapt and change them to incorporate what feels comfortable for you.

Stop Negative Thinking with a Trigger

One way to eliminate negative thinking is with a trigger or cue. Each time you feel a negative emotion such as anger, fear, dislike, or boredom, the trigger makes you aware of the feeling. Then, recognizing the feeling, detach yourself from it, remind yourself you are in control of your feelings, and act to make a change. Just about anything can be a trigger—an object, a word, or a physical motion. One motion that is easy to use is a special, but unnoticeable, hand gesture. Simply touch your thumb to your third finger as a reminder that you are feeling something negative and that you want to get rid of or transform that feeling. The advantage of an unobtrusive hand movement is that you can use it immediately wherever you are, whereas an object may not always be accessible and a word might be blotted out by your negative thoughts. But feel free to use whatever works for you. The key is to build up an association between that physical movement, object, or word so whenever you use it, it blocks your negative feeling and thinking.

To build this association, practice conditioning yourself to make a connection between the trigger and paying attention to a negative feeling. One way to create this association is to take a few minutes each day for about a week or two to focus on the trigger you want to use to alert yourself to a negative feeling. First you must decide on your trigger. Then take a minute to concentrate on this gesture, object, or word and associate it with any negativity you are experiencing, and remind yourself that whenever you are experiencing any negativity you will immediately pull this trigger. Then when you pull this trigger you will be able to remove yourself from the negative feeling you are experiencing. Use your trigger and say to yourself, *I don't want to feel this way.*

To build up the association and practice using your trigger, think of something that annoys you, makes you angry, or makes you feel negative in any way. Then, as soon as this thought comes to you, pull your trigger and notice that your trigger stops the negative thought. Try another negative thought or image, and again pull the trigger. Do this a few more times and tell yourself that in the future any time you experience anything negative you will pull the trigger to make yourself aware, so you can step outside that feeling and stop it. Once you have built this association, whenever you feel negative about something simply pull the trigger and stop the feelings and thoughts.

Say you feel yourself getting angry in a confrontation with someone and you're about to hurl an insult or you feel like hitting the person. Use your trigger instead. You'll feel a sense of detachment and will calm down. Or say you are feeling sad and depressed. Pull the trigger to step outside yourself and detach from those unhappy feelings. To help you gain this detachment, remind yourself that those feelings are separate from you and that you can control them, but that you can now do something different to make the bad feelings go away. As soon as you sense negative feelings coming on, pull the trigger to stop those feelings from coming and send them away.

Clear Out Negativity with Mental Cleansing

Once you realize you are experiencing negative feelings or thoughts, or are around someone who is negative, you can get rid of those negative experiences with a simple mental cleansing technique. Initially a physical action works well since it is more concrete and dramatic. Later, you can create a visualization of yourself cleaning out this negativity. You can use this visualization at any time, unlike a physical gesture that might be out of place. Practice this technique for a week or two until it becomes second nature. Then repeat this exercise whenever you want to physically cleanse yourself of negative feelings.

Stand or sit up straight. Imagine you are in a shower and run your hands over the top of your head and down your neck. As you do this motion, imagine that you are cleaning off any negativity you are experiencing. Feel that negativity coming out of you and into your hands. Take your hands away from your neck and shake out the negativity. Imagine it dissipating into the air and disappearing. Repeat this process a few times—move your hands from the top of your head to your neck then shake them out in a quick, sweeping gesture. Each time you do, more and more negativity is drawn away from you and disappears into the air.

Next, take your right hand and sweep it down your left shoulder and left arm. As you do, imagine any negativity within you going into your hand and shake it out. Feel the negativity being shaken away. Now, take your left hand and sweep it down your right shoulder and right arm and shake that negativity away too. Repeat this process a few times so you feel all the negativity drawn away from these parts of your body.

Finally, using your right hand sweep any negativity from your left side and thigh and down to your knee. Using your left hand, sweep any negativity from your right side and thigh down to your knee. Repeat these steps a few times. When you're finished you should feel clean and refreshed and all the negativity should be gone.

Turn Your Negatives into Positives

Another way to get rid of negative attitudes and feelings, once you have identified them, is to turn them around by asking yourself what you can do to create the opposite positive outlook or feeling. Suppose you feel discouraged because you failed to get a desired job or promotion. Instead of feeling discouraged, ask yourself what you can do to change that feeling. For example, in a relaxed state ask yourself, *What can I do to build myself up?* Or, *What can I do to feel a sense of accomplishment?* After asking your question, remain in this relaxed state and listen for an answer, and do it—or imagine yourself doing it.

In some cases, the response to your question will be something you realistically can do and it makes sense to do it. If you can't reasonably act on the response, however, visualize yourself doing it. The effect will be much the same and your negative feelings will drain away, transformed by your creative positive thinking. The following exercise will help you make this transformation. Practice the process and later you can use it in response to any situation in which you feel negative.

Find a quiet place where you can be alone. If you are experiencing negative feelings about anything in your life now, practice using those feelings. Otherwise, think of a negative incident in your past.

Concentrate on the experience for a minute or two and ask yourself, *What bothers me about the incident?* Or, *What makes me feel so bad about what happened?* Listen to the answer. Whatever happened, identify the basic problem causing the negative feelings. Then ask yourself one or more of the following questions:

- What can I do to turn the situation around?

- What can I do to feel better?

- How would I do things differently if I did it again?

- What can I learn from what happened to make things better in the future?

The particular situation will determine what question to ask, or you may want to ask several questions. Then, without trying to consciously answer the question, listen to your inner voice. It will tell you what you need to do. It may take some time to get an answer, but be patient. Just listen and wait for something to come. If nothing comes, repeat your question or try a different one. When you get your answer, if it's something you can and want to do, do it immediately or as soon as possible. Taking this action will help you turn your negative feelings into positive ones. If the answer is something you can't or don't want to do, visualize yourself doing it.

In either case, this exercise will help you release the negative feelings you have built up around a situation and will help you create new, more positive feelings around the experience you have put in its place. Then, this more positive outlook will help you in getting what you want.

Affirming Negatives Away

Another way to get rid of negative thoughts and feelings is with positive affirmations—positive statements made in the present tense to assert that something is so, such as, *I'm skilled and confident and know I will reach my goal.* When you use affirmations, choose those that are as opposite to the negative thought or feeling you are experiencing as possible. You'll find they're a quick remedy that you can use at any time, unlike visualizations, which require more time and an opportunity to be alone.

To make affirmations most effective, repeat them to yourself again and again so they become etched in your unconscious, or inner mind, and become part of you. You might want to write them on cards and put them in your wallet, in a desk drawer, on a mirror, on a wall, or in another place where you will see them regularly. Here are some affirmations you can use to counter typical negative situations. You can use these or create your own to counteract something negative you have experienced.

- I feel enthusiastic, excited, and upbeat.

- I feel optimistic and certain I will get what I want.

- I know exactly what I am doing. I feel completely confident and sure about myself.

- I know I have the power to earn all the money I need.

- I have some great people and associates around me.

- I know I am doing a good job and others will recognize my contributions.

- I will complete everything I need to do in time to make the deadline.

- I like my job and find the work interesting and challenging.

- I know I am making/have made the right choice. I don't have to apologize for my choice to anyone or feel guilty for having made it. I am doing/have done the right thing.

As an added bonus, use affirmations even when you don't feel negative to increase your feelings of confidence, recommit yourself to a goal, strengthen your sense of personal identity, and generally feel upbeat.

You can use these affirmations by themselves or combine them with other techniques, such as a trigger or a cleansing technique. The advantage of combining these approaches is that after you have acted to stop or chase away the negativity, you add something positive to fill the gap created by its absence, making the negativity less likely to return.

Part Three

The Building Blocks of GWYW Success

Chapter Seven

☙

Increasing Confidence and Self-Esteem

Being confident and using "I can" thinking is one of the keys to getting what you want in life. As you get what you want, you feel more confident and have more self-esteem. It's a reciprocal process that starts with building confidence, although often when people are just starting out in something, they don't feel confident, which can create problems. For when you don't have confidence in yourself, it's easy for others to break you down with the slightest criticism about you or what you're doing. Without a firm sense of self, you can easily agree with them and tear yourself down rather than viewing any criticism objectively as an opinion about your behavior rather than a critique of yourself. The advantage of seeing things objectively is that you can turn any criticism into a chance to change and grow if you feel the criticism is warranted, or disregard it as an observation you don't agree with if you feel the criticism is wrong. When you feel confident you also put aside the "I can't" thinking that is a barrier to getting something when you really can.

Change Your Self-Image to Change Your Life

I know many people who were able to turn their lives around and become successful in their careers by starting with a change in attitude. They started off feeling unsure of themselves and ended up feeling confident by focusing on their good qualities, seeing themselves as successful, and visualizing themselves being prosperous and recognized by others for their efforts and achievements. This approach works because if you believe you are great, you are great! If you believe you can, you probably do what is necessary so you really can. You need to start out with the "I can, I will, or I deserve" beliefs first because that helps to create the experiences you have that support this belief. For example, if you are convinced you should have a certain job or promotion, you'll exude an aura of confidence and act like you belong in that job so people will think of you in that role. Also, with that belief you'll know you can do whatever is required and will be able to do it. And soon you'll find you have that job as you create the reality to reflect your belief.

Certainly, external circumstances and the luck of being in the right place at the right time can also help you gain confidence. For example, I gained more confidence when I was starting out designing games that were later published in the late-1960s as people told me they liked my ideas. But if you lack inner self-assurance, all the luck and favorable circumstances won't give you that feeling of personal power you need to keep things going well for you. Think of the many people who get promoted to a new position at work and for various reasons find they can't handle the additional responsibilities. In effect, it's the Peter Principle in operation, which is the principle that people get promoted until they reach their level of incompetence. Underlying the operations of this principle are the old attitudes some people bring to a new position. Whether consciously or unconsciously, they still see themselves in their old role and don't truly feel confident to expand their levels of performance. They feel they don't deserve promotions or are unworthy. As a result they eventually screw up so they can drop back down to where they feel comfortable. By contrast, when you feel that inner confidence you have that "I can do it whatever it is" feeling and you're ready to take on new tasks and responsibilities and grow. Because you believe you can do it, you can! It all comes down to belief. You must believe you have the power to create the success you want. Then that belief will give you the power you need to do it.

Changing Yourself to End a Relationship

By changing her perception of herself, Joan gained the confidence to end a bad relationship and begin anew. She worked at a series of secretarial and paralegal jobs and was married to her college sweetheart, although now she felt stifled. She had many creative ideas for new fashions and a strong desire for freedom, but her husband kept discouraging her aspirations. He told her about all the ways she could fail and how he was already making good money. So she squelched her aspirations because of her fear that she didn't have the ability to do what she wanted in her present comfortable and unsatisfied life. Instead of breaking away to do what she really wanted, she kept telling herself, *I can't.*

After several years of muddling through, she took a workshop where she learned how to imagine what she wanted and affirm that she could get it. In her imagination there were no barriers. There were no thoughts of *I can't* and no reasons why she couldn't achieve all she desired. Instead, everything she wanted was right there and she merely had to think out the steps she needed to take to begin the process, such as deciding to leave her husband, finding a new place and new job in another city, making a few designs until she had enough clients to quit, and developing a portfolio of photographs so others could show her work to sell it. Thus, instead of thinking of the self-created barriers that prevented her from changing direction in life, Joan began creatively thinking of what she needed to do right now to get the process into motion. As a result she immediately told her husband she had to make the break, as much as she cared for him and appreciated his support, and she immediately began working toward changing her life by moving, finding a new job, and creating designs to make her goal happen. Her feelings of frustration turned into feelings of fulfillment because she was doing what she wanted, which started with simply changing her initial belief in herself. It took gaining those feelings of self-worth and self-esteem to make the break so she could find independence and work toward her goal.

Changing Your Attitude to Change a Job

In another case, Frank was a bookkeeper in a small management consulting company and changed his attitude and gained a new job. He repeatedly felt he had been passed over unfairly in the company's last several salary reviews. He believed he deserved a raise and he was particularly resentful because other employees with the company for less time had gotten raises, sometimes with more impressive job titles. For several months Frank suffered in silence and then went to a class incorporating GWYW techniques. He started thinking about all of his good qualities and how his skills were important to his employers. He also considered what he must do to make his employers value his skills more, and he realized that they placed a strong emphasis on how their management people looked at work. Thus, he realized he needed to upgrade his image by getting some sharper-looking clothes. Additionally, he imagined himself confidently asking his boss for a raise by explaining why he should get a raise.

Frank practiced these techniques for a week, and as he did he felt more and more confident about what he expected to do. He began to realize he was worth the additional raise, rather than feeling resentful that others got raises when he didn't. Also, he invested in a suit and tie that gave him a more authoritative look. With his new assurance and recognizing his greater self-worth, Frank approached his boss. He began talking about his worth to the company, how he had shown his commitment and loyalty over the years, how be believed in working out win-win situations, and finally proposed the raise. Frank not only got his raise but he also got a promotion within a few days. His boss suddenly saw Frank in a new light and was impressed. He realized that

Frank could do more than he was doing and gave him new responsibilities to match.

The change in Frank's life had come about due to an attitude shift first. Frank had looked within himself to develop more confidence and feelings of self-worth. Then those feelings had translated into change in the everyday world.

How to Build Up Your Confidence and Self-Esteem

The key to building up your confidence and self-esteem and overcoming fears, anxieties, self-doubts, and limiting beliefs is to focus on what you can do, know you can do it, and see yourself doing it. Then, using these GWYW techniques, you can reverse those fears and anxieties, and achieve the needed confidence to meet the challenges you face successfully and feel good again. In fact, you can prevent any fears about yourself from creeping into your life by using these methods on a regular basis to affirm that you have the ability to do whatever you want. Further, you can use these techniques to feel confident because you are fully in charge of the situation. The five key ways to build your esteem are:

1) Become aware of and acknowledge your good qualities, talents, and accomplishments.

2) Affirm that you have the qualities you want to develop and keep affirming this as you work on developing these qualities.

3) Visualize yourself as a successful person achieving a goal or being recognized for your efforts.

4) See yourself as a prosperous, abundant person with everything you want.

5. Feel confident, self-assured, and in charge wherever you are.

Recognize Your Good Qualities

Thinking about what you do well is a form of self-affirmation that builds confidence and makes you feel good. Sometimes, you can forget about your good qualities and talents or don't give yourself sufficient credit for how much you have already accomplished. This happens particularly when you encounter difficulties and challenges in life. To counteract such anxieties, you need to remind yourself of what you have and what you can do from time to time. This shores up your self-image and helps you feel surer of yourself again as you think, *I did it in the past. I have the ability to do it, so I can do it now!* The following technique is a good way to start thinking positively.

Get a sheet of paper and a pencil, divide the paper into three columns, and head each one: My Good Qualities, What I Can Do Well, and What I Have Accomplished. Then close your eyes and meditate on each heading separately for a minute or two. What pops into your mind? Don't analyze or question what comes. Just pay attention. After you feel you are finished, open your eyes and write down your good qualities, talents, and accomplishments as quickly as possible. List any new ones that occur to you while you write.

Review your list. As you read each item, create a mental picture of yourself with that quality, talent, or accomplishment. See yourself with all of these qualities, talents, and accomplishments and experience how good this feels. Finally, see yourself being given a blue ribbon and pat yourself on the back to give yourself recognition. You really are first class. You've got a lot going for you and you deserve to compliment yourself for this.

Affirm Yourself and Your Talents

If you are what you think, then if you think positively you'll feel positively. Likewise, if you think you have certain qualities and talents, then you will have them. Even if you don't have these characteristics now, if you think you have them, you'll develop them and your self-esteem will soar. In short, affirm what you want to get and truly feel and believe what you affirm. The following technique will help you do that.

Write down your affirmations about who you are or want to be and about what you have or want. Choose whatever is important to you and affirm it in the present tense even if you don't have that thing or quality now. For example, you might affirm that:

- I have a wonderful, loving family with great (parents, children, mate, etc.).
- I have a winning smile and outgoing personality.
- I have a few really good friends I can count on when needed.
- I can be the life of the party when I want to be.
- I have a great sense of humor and people love to laugh at my jokes.
- I have an exciting, challenging job that I really enjoy.
- I am an exciting, dynamic person and can keep an audience excited about everything I say.
- I am successful in whatever I do and now I am successfully completing a project at work.
- I am prosperous and abundance comes to me.

After you finish writing, select your most important affirmation and focus on it for about a minute. Then, close your eyes and repeat your affirmation over and over to yourself for two to three minutes. As you do this, see the statement you have written in your mind's eye. Don't just hear or see the words, but translate your message into a visual image. Do this daily for about a week and you'll notice that you feel more confident and the things you want will start coming into your life.

For example, when a woman wanted to get more focused on affirming herself as a magnet who attracted people to her, she found she felt more comfortable meeting people at networking events and parties, and she soon had a growing circle of friends. A sales professional who focused on being more successful at her job increased her monthly earnings. A management consultant who concentrated on being a successful speaker started getting paid speaking engagements after several months of free talks for local civic groups. An administrative assistant who found her job dull concentrated on affirming that she had an exciting, challenging job and found a part-time research opportunity that turned into a full-time job.

These affirmations worked because the process led to a subtle attitude change that affected the way they felt about themselves, and in some cases led them to go outside their comfort zone to engage in new and more fulfilling activities. This attitude change and new way of behaving led others to perceive and respond to them differently. You can make this technique work for you to get what you want in the same way.

Visualize Yourself as a Success

As success builds self-esteem, visualizing yourself successful helps you feel more self-assured. This process works because you not only make yourself more aware of opportunities to be successful, but also by seeing yourself as a success you feel what it is like to experience it. You feel more powerful, more dynamic, more directed, and increase your self-recognition, and all of these feelings contribute to you being more confident. You are using mental imagery to convince yourself that you are experiencing what you want in the here and now, and your feelings and actions respond to complement and reinforce that mental image. I have met dozens of people who have done this in many workshops I attended. Typically, they attended the workshops because they were feeling uncertain about their goals in life and lacked a sense of assurance about themselves and what they were doing. But by focusing on and visualizing the success they wanted, they experienced transformations in their lives. They usually returned to the workshop or a follow-up session a week later reporting glorious changes that made them feel more powerful and confident about their abilities to create the experiences they wanted.

For example, Madge was a dental assistant and reported having the confidence to quit and do what she really wanted: open a dress design company. Paul was a computer analyst who felt discouraged that his company didn't take his ideas for new software programs seriously. He felt empowered to push for his ideas more strongly, leading him to get important advocates for his ideas in the marketing department. Judy was an executive assistant who followed her parents' prescription for her future by getting engaged to a businessman and family friend she didn't love. She felt a new determination to stand up to her parents and tell them and her fiancé that this marriage wasn't right for her. She felt confident that she could either find a better match for herself through dating, or if she didn't, she had the confidence to build a life for herself living alone.

The following exercise will give you a taste of having the type of success you want. Repeat this exercise regularly for several days to reinforce this successful image and strengthen your feelings of self-esteem. Later you can turn these feelings into reality by initiating new actions for success or by responding effectively to opportunities that come up.

Begin by deciding what sort of success is most important to you: performing well on your job, getting a larger house, starting a new company, finding a new relationships, or anything else you are hoping for. Next relax, close your eyes, and see yourself realizing this goal.

Make your image of this achievement as vivid as possible and see your success happening in the here and now. For example, if your goal is to perform well at work, see the job fully completed and done perfectly. If your goal is closing a big deal, see yourself making the pitch that results in the sale and see yourself shaking hands after signing the contract. If your goal is getting a bigger office, see yourself sitting in it and talking to clients. If you seek a better relationship, see yourself meeting this person and going on fun-filled dates together. As you visualize your success, experience the satisfaction and feeling of power this brings. Feel elated, excited, strong, powerful, fully self-confident, and in charge. Then see others come up to you or call to congratulate you and feel warm and glowing as you receive their praise. They tell you how successful you are or they compliment you on your great relationship. And you feel wonderful and able to do anything you want.

See Yourself as an Abundant, Prosperous Person

Being abundant and prosperous goes hand in hand with success. It's a symbol of having achieved a desired goal, of gaining fame and recognition, or having power. It's a confirmation and validation of having made it. Whereas the success pictured in the previous exercise represented attaining a goal, the image of prosperity in this exercise represents the rewards of that accomplishment. In turn, concentrating on this prosperity helps you develop the appropriate state of mind for receiving these rewards and attracting them to you in the same way that imagining attaining a goal creates a mind-set that leads you to act or react to achieve it. As you experience this mind-set and concentrate on prosperity as your deserved reward this will add to your feelings of confidence and personal power.

To feel this abundance and prosperity use the symbols of the rewards of success that are important to you. For example, if living a rich and glamorous lifestyle is important, use symbols of this lifestyle such as having money, owning a nice home or car, and traveling in style to interesting places to help achieve it. If your ideal is being a person with popularity and power, visualize images of that such as having an entourage of people around you, giving a speech before an audience of thousands, or arriving at a gala opening as the press snaps photos of your arrival. To feel prosperous choose the images of success you identify with, for you are using your power to visualize the type of success you want to give you the success feeling.

The following techniques will help you develop this abundant, prosperous state of mind. As you go about your daily routine think of these images and feelings from time to time, and you'll feel more confident and be more aware of and receptive to any opportunities to help you become successful. In a short time you'll find money, other forms of prosperity, more relationships, or a more fulfilling relationship developing for you, sometimes in unexpected ways.

Multiplying Your Assets

This technique is designed to make you more aware of the possibilities for increasing your assets in the near future. It suggests the avenues through which you might receive more money.

To begin, take the largest bill you have from your billfold. Then, holding it before you, concentrate on it for about two minutes. As you do notice its colors and its textures. Hold it in different ways in your hand. Meanwhile, think to yourself, *This bill is multiplying itself. There are many more of these coming my way.* Also imagine this bill increasing in value. If it is a one dollar bill, see it as a five dollar bill; if it is a five dollar bill, see it as ten dollars; if it is a ten dollar bill, see it as twenty dollars; and so on. Meanwhile thinking, *I'm not limited to what I have. I can increase the value of my money at any time.* Still holding the bill, ask yourself, *How might more money come to me?* and wait for a mental image to form. It might be of you in a new job, handling a new project, starting a new business, or being paid for speaking to a group. Then ask again, *How else might this come to me?* and wait for another image. Keep asking this question and waiting for images until the images stop coming freely. At the same time, feel the power you have to increase the money coming to you.

Later you can use the information from this experience to make changes in your life to increase your assets if it is necessary. Or use the feeling of confidence and power gained by the exercise to be more aware of opportunities to increase your income in everyday life.

Picture Your Prosperity

Whether you want a better job, a bigger business, or anything else, this technique will help you focus on your goal. In turn, the positive energy you direct toward this objective will help you mobilize your inner forces to attain it. This exercise involves creating a visual image to make your thoughts and desires more concrete, which will make them stronger and more powerful. The process works the same way as writing down goals. It makes them more real so you're not just casually dreaming about something, but you're working on actualizing the results you want. You're taking steps to make sure what you want really happens.

To prepare, either draw or cut out a picture of what you want from a newspaper or magazine. You can also cut out words or phrases that express your goals. Use an image or set of words that are as close to what you want as possible. Now glue this picture on a sheet of cardboard. Decorate it as attractively as possible using magic marker, drawings, and whatever else you would like. Perhaps frame it or surround it with a gold border. When you are finished, place a small picture of yourself in the center of this image. Then, holding this image in front of you, concentrate on it for several minutes. See yourself getting what you want and direct a stream of positive energy from your mind into this image. If you feel you need additional energy, draw it into yourself from the earth or from the air around you. Visualize the earth energy coming up through your feet and spine to your head, and see energy from the air coming down into your head. Direct this energy into the image.

Spend about three minutes focusing your inner forces in this way and, as you do, imagine that you have achieved everything illustrated in the images or words you picture. Afterward, keep this picture around your house or office where you can see it from time to time as a reminder of your expected prosperity. Preferably, put it where others won't see it to better preserve the specialness of this image and give it more power.

Affirm Your Prosperity

To reinforce these prosperity techniques, affirm your growing abundance from time to time. You can do this wherever you are—waiting in line, on a bus, in an airplane, or wherever. In fact, when you feel especially under pressure or irritated about something, this affirmation is a good way to perk up your spirits and help you feel secure and confident again.

Just repeat to yourself for a minute or so, *I am abundant, I am prosperous. I am rich and have all the money I need and want.* When you stop, feel a flow of abundance, well-being, and power surge through you. Feel like you have everything you want and can use that to do anything you wish.

Feel Confident Wherever You Are

The final step to being fully confident is feeling as if you are fully in control and in charge wherever you are. Affirming your abilities and talents and seeing yourself as an abundant, successful person helps to give you that feeling. In addition, you can increase these powerful, in-charge feelings by using mental imagery to remind yourself that you are these things. The following technique is designed to give you the experience of being in control wherever you are. Stay fully alert as you use this technique, which includes holding a mental image of being fully in charge of the situation. This "control of the room" approach uses one take-charge image, but you can use any image that feels comfortable for you.

Know that you can feel confident and self-assured wherever you are. To do this, as you enter an area, imagine a force field of powerful energy radiating out from your head to the four corners of the room. At the same time, imagine a column of energy beaming down into your head from above you and flowing down along your spine and through your feet. This column of energy makes you feel strong and solid while the force field that radiates out from you gives you control of wherever you are. As you walk about and talk to people, feel this energy or force move with you. It remains around you, protecting you, providing assurance and control, and is constantly replenished from the energy beaming into you. Once you know this energy is around you, you no longer need to focus on it. Should you feel your assurance or control of any situation weaken, imagine that you are sending out additional force to the four corners of the room and re-experience the strong energy from the earth and air around you flowing through you and recharging you with its strength.

Turning Your I Can'ts into I Cans

Another way to build confidence and self-esteem is to dig more deeply to get rid of the *I can'ts* that are standing in the way and turn them into *I cans*. It's a way to feeling more confident and powerful by becoming the best you can be at something. Athletes, chess champions, and any other competitors who succeed not only start with an inner talent or predisposition and work hard to make it happen, but also have a powerful belief in themselves and the motivation to focus that into a superior performance. They have what is sometimes called having fire in the belly—the drive that inspires one to go the distance burning in their gut. Fueling this fire is the burning mental desire, drive, or inner passion to do it combined with the belief of "I can and I will."

This drive can break through the barriers that can stand in the way of achievement and can help you uncover hidden skills and talents that might otherwise lie dormant. The process is like when a bomber flies through flak and enemy fire to achieve its objective. The flak is the personal I can'ts, and the enemy fire are the external obstacles that slow you down or stop you along the way. But, like the bombers, if you press on, skillfully avoiding the flak and the fire, fueled by your inner desire and with a focus on the target that represents your will, you can do it. So to realize your goal, keep that desire channeled into action. At the same time, maintain a belief in yourself, have the will to do it, and keep your focus on the goal. Dodge the I can'ts and external obstacles, or keep them out of the way.

Discovering the Source of I Can't Messages to Get Rid of Them

I can't messages are among the biggest obstacles to becoming your best or overcoming everyday problems you encounter. But if everyday problems, obstacles, and challenges are turned into opportunities for learning and growth they become positive experiences. I can't messages block the way and confirm themselves. If you think you can't do it, you probably can't. In turn, if you think you can, you probably can.

These messages frequently start in childhood. Parents often convey these messages because they want to protect their child; afraid they can't meet the challenge and will be hurt or feel put down in trying. They fear letting the child even try. They say no and urge the child to do something else by using the excuses "You can't" or "You're not old enough," or something similar. While such messages are necessary, sometimes to keep children from real dangers, a parent's knee-jerk urge to say no to their child contributes to future I can't thinking. If a child hears these negative messages often enough, they become internalized and block out valuable learning experiences. Later, they can hold a person back from doing something he or she really wants because the person thinks *I can't* when he or she really can if they let go of that message.

When I was a child, I found myself fighting back against I can't messages from my parents, and when I found I *could* I gained the confidence to fight against other I can't messages that came my way. One of my earliest experiences of this occurred when I was seven or eight years old in summer camp. My parents had signed me up for horseback riding lessons, and like several other children, I had trouble learning to ride. We fell off a few times, and after a couple of potentially dangerous falls the counselors decided we shouldn't take any more lessons. That was probably a safe decision, but I was determined to learn to ride. A few days later I sneaked back into the class. No one noticed and this time I was so determined to stay on the horse that I did. By the time the counselors discovered me, I had proven I could do it and they let me stay in the class. Because I didn't let their I can't messages stop me, I discovered that I could and grew more confident about trying other activities.

As I grew up, I found the experience of overcoming the I can'ts and discovering the I cans helped set the stage for future encounters. My parents, particularly my mother, kept saying, "You can't do well in this course, handle this difficult job, succeed in this new place," and so on. But having the will and the fire to do it, I did them anyway. I was eager to try new things. I wanted to overcome, not shrink back from, the challenges, and I accomplished them.

Getting from I Can't to I Can and I Will

By contrast, I have met many people who have been held back by I can't thinking, so they do or become much less than they could. Afraid to try and fail, they don't try even though they probably could have succeeded if they did. Some are held back by the fear of not being perfect—if they can't be the absolute best very quickly, they feel there's no point in doing something at all. By setting impossible standards for themselves they don't try, so they don't fail, but they miss the point. The goal is not to be the absolute best in something, but to be your personal best, so you can do and be the best you possibly can at what you want to do. What gives the feeling of exhilaration and empowerment is maximizing personal expression and attainment, not struggling to meet some abstract, impersonal standard set by someone else. By confronting I can't thinking, often you find you can, but doing so can sometimes be very scary. You have to give up a comfortable habit. It also takes repeated practice to change what you are used to doing and feeling, but after a while, by working on reprogramming your attitude and forcing yourself to do what you want but fear you can't, you will find you can do it.

Moreover, when you turn I can't into I can in one area of your life, this I can approach will carry over into other areas as well.

I experienced this myself. When I was growing up I was afraid of taking on a leadership role or being in charge of anything because my mother had been a very demanding, domineering person and she used her power to put down others to do what she wanted. I sensed their resentment and didn't want to be like that. So I soon turned my resistance to taking on a leadership role into a message that "I can't do this." But then I encountered several situations where I had to take on such a role in order to get things done. I began forcing myself to take on this role, such as facilitating focus groups at work when an outside professional wasn't available, or instructing the assistant in what to do when the department manager was out of town. And later, as a teaching assistant in graduate school, I pushed through my fears to act like a confident, knowledgeable TA. Within a few minutes, the feelings of anxious uncertainty were gone and I was playing the role I had to assume as being a grad student. Subsequently, I used these same techniques to apply for and get a job as an assistant professor, as well as do research as a participant observer in several groups where I had to lead group sessions. So eventually, by taking on each challenge in this can do spirit, I ended up with several published books on different groups based on my experiences as a participant observer. By getting rid of the I can'ts, focusing on the I cans by visualizing myself doing what I wanted to do, and practicing doing it despite my initial feelings of resistance and anxiety, I was able to push aside the barriers and get what I wanted.

I have met many others who have likewise turned their can'ts into cans. The key to achieving their goal was an attitude change: this can do belief that motivated them to stick to whatever they were doing and to achieve.

Eliminating the Critical—
Accentuating the Supportive

An I can approach can be reinforced by not letting the negative thinking or critical judgments of others get you down, and by not engaging in the "What will others think" syndrome. When you compare yourself to others and think, *I can't be as good*, it is just another way of putting yourself down. Of course, most of us can't succeed if we try to achieve professional standards without the necessary training, or try to measure ourselves against someone with years of practice when we're just beginning. We each start with our own special combination of talents, skills, and interests, but then generally need additional training to accomplish certain tasks. If you don't get this training, or if you do but set unrealistic standards of achievement for yourself, you're setting yourself up to fail and reinforcing your belief that you can't. Certainly select a successful role model as an inspiration to learn from and follow as a guide, but then think of what you can do as you.

Jeremy was an artist and got trapped in the cycle of comparing himself to others, failing, and concluding I can't. He was unable to succeed at what he really wanted because he was so afraid he couldn't measure up to the artists he admired. Though he was an excellent artist and photographer, he was afraid to enter competitions or take his work around to the galleries because he couldn't face the prospect of being turned down. He remained stuck in jobs instead of pursuing more demanding and lucrative opportunities, and he expressed his frustration by badmouthing many of the artists who got ahead. But he never recognized how his own can't do thinking of comparing himself to others stalled his career and fueled his bitterness. As a result, he essentially sabotaged himself by being so afraid that he couldn't that he acted as if he couldn't, and therefore, that became a self-fulfilling prophecy. Had he changed his attitude, he could have taken the steps necessary to succeed.

Some Exercises and Techniques for Changing I Can'ts into I Cans

The following exercises and techniques are designed to empower you to change your I can't messages into I cans. They will help you to recognize the I can'ts that are holding you back, decide which ones you want to eliminate first, decide what you can do to change I can'ts into I cans, track your progress in eliminating the I can'ts, and make I can thinking a regular part of your life.

Ways to Change I Can'ts into I Can's

To get rid of the I can'ts you have to first be aware of them and decide which ones to get rid of. This exercise will help you gain this awareness and decide your priorities for changing these can'ts into cans.

Start with a blank sheet of paper and a pencil ready. Write two column headers: What I can't do but want to do, and What I'd like to do if I could. Then close your eyes and get relaxed.

Now, looking at your inner mental screen, ask yourself, *What do I think I can't do that I would like to do?* Then let your imagination go and notice what comes. As you discover each new can't, write it down under the first column. Spend two to three minutes listing your can'ts.

Then ask yourself, *What would I like to do if I could?* Again, let your imagination go and write what comes in the second column. Some answers may be the same, but you may find new ones by phrasing the question in this different way. Spend about two to three minutes doing this.

Now go back over your list and rate those I can'ts and I would like to on a scale of one to five, with one being the top priority and five being the lowest priority, on how important it is to you to change these things. Then select the I can'ts you first want to work on overcoming.

Deciding How to Change the I Can'ts into I Cans

Once you identify the can'ts you want to work on, the next step is deciding what you can do to change them into cans. What resistances or fears are holding you back? What practical steps might you take to overcome any resistances? What might you do to prove you can? What actions should you take now?

Again, close your eyes and get relaxed. Then, focusing on each I can't you selected to change into an I can, ask the following questions. Let the answers come to you and write them down.

- What resistances or fears are holding me back? Why do I feel I can't do this?

- Are there any other resistances or fears I may have?

- Is there anything I haven't noticed or don't want to notice?

Now that you have listed any resistances or fears, ask yourself what you might do to overcome them and change that can't into a can. This time see what ideas come to you when you are in a receptive mode with your eyes closed. Then try brainstorming in a more active mode with your eyes open. Again, write down what you might do. For example, if you have a fear of speaking, your list of resistances and fears and your list of what you can do might look something like this:

Resistances and Fears	What I Might Do
Looking foolish	Join Toastmasters
Forgetting what I want to say	Volunteer to conduct interviews
Not being good enough	Practice in front of my mirror
Being embarrassed	Speak into my tape recorder
Being boring	Go door-to-door in a political campaign

After identifying the things you might like to do, go back over the list and rate them again from one to five, with one having the top priority and five having the lowest, to show what you would most like to put into practice now. Start doing that within the next day or two.

Charting Your Progress

As you work on discovering and eliminating your can'ts it helps to chart your achievements along the way. It generally takes about three weeks to get rid of a habit, so figure it will take you about this long to change your I can't approach into an I can attitude. Charting your achievements not only lets you know how you are doing, but it also helps to set up milestones and show points along the way where you can reward yourself for your achievements. If, for example, you are working on losing weight, you may want to do something special to recognize your achievement every time you lose five pounds. If you are working on overcoming a fear, you might reward each breakthrough with a wonderful meal.

A datebook or daily calendar in either book form or computer program is fine for this purpose. Simply check off each day you have stayed on course or each time you achieved a particular objective. You may want to add comments to yourself such as "Good speech," or "Congratulations at resisting that cake at the office party."

Making I Can Thinking a Part of Your Life

Besides working on overcoming specific I can'ts, you can work on stopping I can't thinking any time you encounter it. For example, when someone asks you to do something or when you are trying something new, do you find yourself saying I can't? If so, ask yourself why you are saying this. Is it because you really don't want to do it because you can't for a real reason, such as a conflict in time or a skill you can't acquire in time, or is a fear or resistance preventing you from doing something you really would like to do?

If the reason is a fear or resistance, try saying, "Yes I can," and do what you need to do to make it happen. If you make I can thinking a habit, you'll find you can do all sorts of interesting and enjoyable things you might otherwise have blocked yourself from experiencing. I can thinking has carried me along many roads. It led to me setting up several sales organizations, which led to my consulting and writing on the subject, which led to a published book and many successful speaking engagements on the topic. It led me to design and market dozens of games. It led me to write songs, books, scripts, produce indie films, and most recently, find a house in Lafayette and move there.

It would have been very easy to say, "No, I've never done this before," at each new hurdle, but by pushing aside my initial I can't fears and simply saying, "Sure, I'll give it a try," I figured out how to do it and did it successfully. By focusing on what to do to make I can happen, not on whether I could, and by acting the role I wanted to play, I became what I wanted to be. By believing I can, I could. As I got to know others in the field of sales and speaking, I realized that many of them had no previous experience either, but they too had become very successful because they believed they could.

Therefore, whenever you face anything new or threatening, notice if you have a tendency to say I can't. It's often just a knee-jerk reaction to the idea of change. If that's your typical response, be aware of it and stop yourself before you tell yourself you can't. Ask yourself if it really is that you can't do something, or do you have a general attitude of resistance or fear that is holding you back? If the latter is the case, don't say I can't right away. Instead say I can, or I'd like to consider it. Then, if you can, and want to, say I can. Once you say that, you'll find the way to make it happen. Saying it will help you believe it, and in turn, will help to make it happen. So say it again and again: I CAN! I CAN! I CAN!

Chapter Eight

꩜

Creating the Personality and Self-Image You Want

To be successful in a career, business, or personal relationship it helps to have certain personality traits. The ideal traits differ to some extent from occupation to occupation or in different cultures. For instance, a salesperson needs to be an outgoing, assertive, positive, and self-motivated person who takes initiative and is persuasive and articulate. While an office worker should be conscientious, detail oriented, organized, and willing to take orders. In some cultures a woman is expected to be more submissive and nurturing, whereas being assertive and independent is more characteristic of women in the United States and Western Europe. However, some traits are desirable for everyone, such as being a confident, friendly, creative, energetic, and positive person.

Decide the personality traits or self-image best for you and your career or business path, as well as in the type of relationships you want. Then decide if you have the desired personality or self-image, or determine the areas you want to develop further to get closer to your ideal. The results can be dramatic if you decide to make major changes—a job more in line with your abilities and interests, improved job performance and a higher income, more satisfying relationships, or more personal power at work and at home.

Personality and Job Changes

These examples illustrate how personality changes can lead to great personal success and a greater fit between the work one is currently doing and the work one wants to do.

From Accountant to Confident Marketer

Sam was fairly shy and bookish and worked as an accountant in a high-tech company building space equipment. At work he garnered praise for his quiet persistence, conscientiousness, and precision. So outwardly there was a good fit between the work and the way he behaved. Sam, however, was unsure of himself with people. He felt ill-at-ease going to parties and making small talk. At work this didn't matter because his employers were more interested in his financial skills than how he interacted with others.

For several years nothing changed. Sam imagined that it would be nice to be more outgoing and socially comfortable, but he did nothing about it since he was comfortable in his job. But then, due to cutbacks, Sam suddenly found himself out of work in a market much less receptive to his skills. He had to change, not because he might like to be different, but for his own economic survival. Sam began thinking about the kinds of jobs that were available and realized that he would need to improve his social skills to land one of them. He decided to use his financial skills to market some mortgage and financial services, and began to work on making himself over in order to step into this new role. At first he was nervous about approaching people to sell them anything. But he began imagining himself in this role and practiced at home in front of his mirror. Finally he gained enough confidence to start interviewing and landed a job in telemarketing. Later as he gained more confidence from his success on the phone and his mental visualization and mirror practice at home, he got a job as an outside marketing representative. Gradually he moved from playing the role of an enthusiastic financial services marketing rep to being one.

At the same time, his more outgoing personality characteristics for his new work carried over into his personal life and he was more comfortable in social situations. He had gradually left his shyness behind as he became accustomed to working with people. After a while he was no longer the shy, bookish accountant he had once been. He had become a knowledgeable and friendly financial services rep, and that felt good.

How You Can Make a 180 in Your Personality

Sam's dramatic change from shy introvert to outgoing extrovert illustrates that you can change even your most basic personality traits when necessary. Although we develop certain traits as a result of our experiences we are, in fact, very flexible and can adapt in many ways. Even what may at first seem like a 180-degree transformation may come to seem very natural, and after a while you may be able to shift back and forth between styles, choosing whichever is more appropriate to a particular situation. Or the new trait may virtually replace the older one if we have made permanent changes in our lives. I have met many people who have altered their personalities and self-images for greater success in different ways.

For example, a man who managed a small order processing department realized he was too abrasive in dealing with employees, and he worked on becoming more supportive and finding ways to give praise rather than criticism. As a result he increased his unit's productivity, which then led to a nice raise for himself. An elementary school teacher realized she tended to be impatient and overly critical of people, which made some students resentful and caused them to lose interest in their work. To counteract this, she learned to slow down and become more patient, which resulted in a better behaved class and higher grades for the students.

In still another case, a usually critical woman with a caustic sense of humor realized that what she thought was witty was actually a turn-off for many people. They found her jokes and comments more hurtful than humorous, so she realized she needed to change to become a more caring and compassionate person in order to develop better relationships with others. Eventually, as she changed she found others warmed up to her, and she found more of the men she was attracted to were drawn to her too, so she began dating more.

Changing Your Personality in Different Situations

One way to think about your personality is to see yourself like an actor playing a role where you change your personality to adapt to changing circumstances. You may think you have a set personality, but it's a construct that is continually being reaffirmed or recreated as you interact with others. *Social interactionist* refers to the school of psychologists and social researchers who have found this to be true.

You have probably experienced this personality transformation yourself when you are one way at work, another way at home, and bring out different aspects of yourself with family members and friends. This change occurs because we are constantly playing different roles in different situations with different people. We are tough with some people, while soft and gentle with others. We act like a child with some, like a nurturing parent with others, and like an aggressive drill sergeant with others. Often the situation shapes the role we play—we step into different costumes to take on different roles.

But what about with new people and new situations? What if we have new roles to play and we aren't sure what to do or if we can do it? Or suppose we aren't sure the particular role we have been playing will fly with a new boss, in a new company, or with a new group of people in a social group? There are many occasions when there is an uncertain fit between who we usually are or expect to be and the role required in a new and unfamiliar situation. Take some of these common examples:

- You are asked to take charge and aren't sure what to do.

- You have to make a career change because of changed economic circumstances and the culture of the new field is very different from the one to which you were accustomed.

- You are working with a new group of people who have different values and expectations and you want to get along.

- You want to advance to a new position where you have to take on different tasks and roles.

- You are often critical and demanding, which has led to conflicts with your parents and friends in public places, so you have to learn to chill out and be more accepting of what is.

All such changes mean you must learn to act in a new way, perhaps even change your image and bring out a hidden side of you. You may also want to change to be more like someone you admire or express a hidden side. Or perhaps the way you have been acting isn't working and you want to change it. For example:

- You are too shy and unassertive so people step all over you.

- You are difficult to work with or talk to because you are too sensitive and irritable.

- You are too pushy and aggressive, so people you would like to work with or family members are often afraid of you or try to avoid you.

- You are too critical and judgmental, so close friends and partners clam up on you because they are afraid to tell you information since you tend to criticize what they are doing or give them unwanted advice.

For one reason or another, you need to make some personality changes to alter the way you act or are so you fit in or get along better with people. It sounds difficult, but when you change the results will amaze you. You may get a more satisfying job that you really like, have greater success in working with others, have increased opportunities, better relationships, and numerous other things all because you have learned to be more flexible. The key is to determine the personality traits that no longer work and figure out what qualities you need to adopt to be successful. Then you can work on practicing these new traits

Four Key Stages to Changing Yourself

There are four key stages to changing yourself to become the person you want to be. You start by imagining who you want to be, visualize yourself in the new role using mental scripting, practice mental scripting, and turn the new script for yourself into action. Here's how the four stages work in more detail.

Determine What to Change

Ask yourself, *How would I like to change?* For example, would you like to be more outgoing and dynamic? More warm and affectionate? More articulate? More self-assured in a group? However you want to change, your GWYW abilities can help you imagine the qualities you want to eliminate and those you want to develop.

Script Yourself into a New Role

This procedure lays the groundwork for you to change because you create a new persona or character for yourself, much like an actor might do.

Reinforce Your New Self-Image

By rehearsing your new role over and over again in your mind you reinforce the reality of this new image. So you see yourself differently when you act in the real world, which helps you act differently as well.

Put Your New Script into Action

Take the new role and actions you have created for yourself and put them into practice in real-life situations. For instance, if you decide you want to be more outgoing and have imagined yourself being this way with coworkers or family members, do just that. As you do, keep in mind the image of yourself as a more outgoing, friendly person who evokes positive responses from others.

The following techniques are designed to help you with each phase of this process.

Determining What You Want to Change or Become

The process of creating a new personality or role for yourself is much like the process of getting and achieving goals as was described earlier, except now your goal is to become a different person with different personality characteristics. Start off by thinking about all the personality traits you want to develop. Then decide which qualities are most important to you so you can work on achieving them first. You ask yourself questions like, *How would I like to change?* Or, *What or who do I want to become?* Consider what aspects of your personality you don't like and imagine their opposite. For example, if you feel you are too quiet, think about what it would be like to be more assertive and outgoing. If you feel you are too standoffish and reserved, imagine yourself participating more. If you lack confidence, see yourself as an assured, confident person. Using this technique you change the picture of yourself. You replace the qualities you don't want with a picture of yourself possessing the qualities you do.

To prepare, get a sheet of paper and pencil and make two columns. At the head of one column write down the heading, *The Personality Traits I Want to Eliminate.* At the head of the second column write, *The Personality Traits I Want to Develop.* When you do this technique, list the personality traits you want to change in the first column as they occur to you. Don't try to edit or analyze them. Then in column two, when you list an opposite or different quality, the one you would like to replace the old one with, write down the first quality that comes to mind so you keep your responses spontaneous.

Finally, for each pair create a picture in which you see yourself in a scene with the original quality. Again, let the picture come to you. Then imagine that this picture is suddenly torn up and see yourself with the opposite or different quality. Experience yourself possessing this new quality for about a minute.

Go through the list and select those changes that are most important to you. Repeat the visualizations of yourself first with the old quality, then with the new. Repeat the visualization over the next few days and try putting each one into practice. You can use the following instructions to do this exercise.

Holding the chart you have created in front of you, get in a relaxed frame of mind. Perhaps turn the lights down to help you concentrate, but leave on enough light so you can see to write.

Then, looking at the first column begin brainstorming and quickly list all the traits you want to eliminate. Write down whatever pops into your mind and don't try to judge whether it is realistically possible for you to get rid of that quality or not. Keep going until you have listed at least five traits or have started to slow down.

Next, turning to the second column begin brainstorming and quickly list all the traits you want to acquire. In some cases, these may be the reverse of the traits you want to eliminate. That's fine. Just list whatever comes up without trying to critique or evaluate it. Also, don't try to decide now if it's realistically possible to acquire that quality. Keep going until you have listed at least five traits or have started to slow down.

When you feel finished, you are ready to prioritize the traits you want to eliminate or develop. To do this, first look down the list of traits you want to eliminate, and for each one come up with the complementary trait you would like to acquire and list it in the second column. For instance, if you have listed "become less negative and critical," the complementary trait would be "become more positive and accepting." After you have listed the complementary trait, cross out the trait you want to eliminate. If you have already listed a complementary trait in the second column, cross off the listing in the first column.

To prioritize the traits to acquire, look at each trait on the list and indicate how important it is to you by using the following markers: A (very important), B (important), and C (nice, but not that important). Write the letter next to each quality.

Finally, look at all the traits you have marked with an A. If you have more than one trait in this category, rank them in order of priority starting with the number one and so on. Do the same for the rest of the letters until each trait has a number or letter next to it.

You have now established your priorities. Plan to work on developing your most important quality first. If you have the time and energy, add your second or third traits. But at most, only work on three qualities at a time. Once you feel solid about having made these part of your personality, go on to the next traits on your list in order of priority (taking all the As first in order, then the Bs, and finally the Cs). Or if you feel you have gone through extensive changes, make a new priority list.

Using Mental Scripting to See Yourself in a New Role

Once you have decided which trait or traits to develop first, the next step is using mental scripting to develop them. In mental scripting, you see yourself as you want to be and create a scenario that you can play out again and again in your mind until you have developed the assurance that you can do it. In setting the scene for your scenario, use somewhere that you want to use your new role.

For example, to develop a more assertive, authoritative personality to take over a managerial position in your company, picture yourself being that way in your present position and see others responding to your new image in the appropriate way. This could be having employees listening more seriously or coming to you frequently for advice. Additionally, see yourself being authoritative and assertive in the position you want and notice that people defer to you and respect you. Alternatively, to become a warmer, friendlier person to get along better with coworkers or family members, see yourself doing things in the office or at home to express this warmth and friendliness such as greeting people with a big smile and a friendly comment, or offering hugs to close friends and family members if it seems appropriate. Use your usual relaxed, meditative state to imagine whatever scenario you choose.

Using an Image Reinforcer

Along with seeing yourself in a new role, you can use an image reinforcer such as a color, animal image, or expert as a reminder in a real-life setting to adopt the role you have imagined in your mind. The way to create this reinforcer is to make an association between the role you want to adopt, the way you want to change to suit that role, and the reminder to help you make that change.

Use the image reinforcer that feels most comfortable for you. The three types of images suggested here are a color image, animal image, and expert image. The basic process is the same; what differs is the particular image you use as a reminder to act as you wish according to your mental script.

The Color Imagery Technique

In this technique you imagine a color around your body representing the quality you would like to develop. For example, to be more aggressive, outgoing, or assertive picture an aggressive color such as red. To be warmer and friendlier picture a warm color such as orange. To be more detail oriented and organized use a color associated with intellectual ability such as yellow. Each color is linked to certain common associations or you can choose your color reinforcer based on your own color associations with that quality.

Later, when you are in a real situation and need additional support for your new trait, imagine this color is around you and let it infuse you with energy and confidence to help you play out your new role.

The Animal Imagery Technique

In the animal imagery technique you visualize an animal representing the characteristic you want to acquire. Choose the animal based on your associations with that animal, although there are certain common associations as in the color approach. For example, to be warm and friendly visualize a soft, furry animal like a kitten or a puppy. To be aggressive visualize an active, aggressive animal like a wolf or a fox. To be more articulate, visualize a talkative animal like a dolphin or a parrot.

Later, in the actual situation when you need a reinforcer, call up this animal image so you will feel more confident to act as you wish.

The Expert Imagery Technique

In the expert image technique you imagine yourself as an expert who is supremely skilled in the desired characteristics. Furthermore, you see yourself doing the kinds of things experts commonly do such as talking about a new book on a TV talk show or giving a newspaper interview. For example, if you want to be a better cook at home imagine yourself as one of the star chefs you see on TV. If you want to be more authoritative when you teach or speak about a subject, imagine yourself as an expert in the subject, picking either a real expert or a fictional one as a role model.

Later, in a real situation, you can draw on this image as a reminder of how you want to be.

Using the Image Reinforcer Techniques
to Acquire Specific Personality Traits

The following examples illustrate how to use these image techniques with a scenario to develop a particular trait. These examples are based on some common qualities people seek to acquire for more success in a work situation. To acquire another trait, develop your own scenario around that and feel free to use any reinforcer that you are comfortable with combined with any trait.

Color a More Outgoing, Dynamic You

In this technique, start by imagining yourself in a situation in which you are more the way you want to be—in this case, outgoing and dynamic. Some possibilities include teaching a class, having a better relationship with your partner, or making a sale. See yourself in that situation and mentally play out that role as vividly as you can. Conclude by seeing the color you associate with those qualities, such as red, around you. The following example uses a party. As usual, first close your eyes and relax.

See yourself arriving at the party. You open the door and the event is in full swing. The atmosphere feels charged and full of energy as people move around meeting and greeting each other. People are talking enthusiastically, clinking glasses, laughing, smiling, exchanging cards, or shaking hands. You notice some people near the center of the room who you haven't met before since they are friends of friends or new in town. Without hesitation you go over to them, smile broadly, and say hello. Then you make a comment that draws you instantly into the conversation, such as stating you hadn't met them before, heard they were from out of the area, or new in town and heard them mention a common associate. Whatever it is, you speak with confidence so the others eagerly listen and respond. When you share a story about how you first moved to the area and got to know people, they find your story especially interesting and hope to see you again and get together to go to some fun activity. You conclude the conversation by exchanging phone numbers and e-mails and saying you will be in touch later. Then you politely excuse yourself to move on to the next individual or group. When you do, you feel the same sense of assurance and know exactly what to say.

Spend about five minutes going from group to group in your mind. Then before you leave, stand in the doorway for a moment. As you do, you see a color representing the outgoing and dynamic personality qualities you have displayed. This color may be red or may be another color. It seems to surround you and radiates from you brightly. Experience the strong energy or force radiating from this color for a few moments. This color will remain with you and whenever you want to be more outgoing and dynamic, think of this color. It will appear around you again and give you a renewed charge of energy and self-confidence so you can express these desired traits. When you are ready, leave the party and open your eyes.

If you are in any other situation where you want to develop any personality trait using the color imagery approach, see yourself in this situation and vividly play out the role. Then end your visualization by seeing the color around you. In the actual situation, visualize that color around you, too.

Use Animal Imagery to Create a New You

In the animal imagery technique, first see yourself as an animal representing the qualities you want to develop. With this image in mind, then imagine yourself in a situation where you want to express those qualities. Later, the image will help you do this in real life because you will act from the feelings associated with that image. The following example illustrates how this process might work if you want to improve your relationships with others by becoming more warm and friendly with your neighbors.

Begin by closing your eyes and getting relaxed. See yourself as a soft, gentle, friendly animal like a kitten or puppy. Someone is holding you in their lap and petting you. The strokes feel warm and comforting and you feel cozy, protected. You feel very friendly and show this by alternately stretching and snuggling up in a small, cuddly ball. This person continues to stroke you and you feel very peaceful, trusting, and content.

With this image in mind, see yourself in a situation in which you want to be open and friendly with someone, such as with neighbors. Imagine you meet in an elevator or by your backyard fence. Go up to that person and say something in a friendly, chatty way, certain they will respond in kind. They do so and you talk comfortably for several minutes, talking about the neighborhood and how you might be able to help each other in the future, such as by sharing tools or checking on each other's mail when you are away.

Hold these images in mind for a few minutes and alternately focus on the soft, friendly animal and on the situation you have imagined. When you are in a real situation where you want to be more open and friendly, think of the animal image and it will help you attain this de-sired state. You can use other animal imagery to reinforce other ways of acting as well. For instance, if you expect a tough encounter with someone, a wolf image might make you tougher. If you have to think through a difficult intellectual challenge, a wily fox might help make you more mentally agile. If you are asking for permission to do some-thing perhaps a bear or lion image might give you added confidence.

Whatever the situation, focus on the animal image briefly and then visualize the situation you want to affect. Finally, in the real-life situa-tion recall that animal image to reinforce the way you want to act.

Use Expert Imagery to Become More Articulate

The expert imagery technique is especially apt when you need to feel powerful or be an authority on something. You start off by seeing your-self as an expert in a controlled situation, like a TV talk show or inter-view. Then, if you have a situation that you want to apply this feeling of power or expertise to, you see yourself in that situation being effective and in charge. If you have no particular situation in mind and simply want to acquire an air of authority and expertise, just see yourself as an expert. The last phase is applying this image in everyday life. You recall your image of you as the expert as a reminder that you can talk knowledgeably and confidently about the subject at hand.

To begin, close your eyes and relax. Now see yourself as an expert of a subject. You have just written a book about it and are a guest on a talk show. You feel calm and comfortable. You know your subject matter perfectly and are ready to answer any questions. The cameras start rolling and your host begins the interview. How did you come to write your book? Where did you get your material? Why do you feel your book has been successful? What do you think of such and such? What advice would you give others? And so on. As you answer each question, your host listens attentively and seems impressed by your wide knowledge of your field. Keep talking and answering questions for several minutes. Be aware of how good it feels to be so knowledgeable and to express what you think and feel.

Now, if there is a situation in life where you want to be regarded as an expert or authority, see yourself in that situation. You have just left a very successful national tour as an expert and you bring that expertise and assurance to this situation. Whatever the situation may be, see yourself responding knowledgeably and confidently just as you did on the talk show. Later in a real-life situation, recall this image of yourself as the expert and know that you are able to talk knowledgeably and with complete assurance about your topic.

Control the Different Aspects of You

Another way to create a change in your personality is to know when to use the traits you have. To do this you need to be aware of when you are expressing different traits so you can use each of them more appropriately. It's not that the trait doesn't fit the situation and that you have to develop the opposite trait. Rather you need to be able to control the use of the trait that works in certain contexts and use a different trait in others. This allows you to respond at your best to the wide range of situations you confront in your daily life.

That's what Paul, the coordinator of a large volunteer organization, was able to do. The members really loved him because he was kind and caring. They also liked his casual spontaneity that helped people feel immediately at ease. At the same time, these traits sometimes led to problems. Paul had trouble managing the group and was often too nice, spontaneous, and disorganized. Since he wanted so much to help people and be liked, he sometimes lacked the discipline necessary to control the group. At one point he even tried an experiment in democracy that led some members of the group to rebel and try to run the program themselves.

Paul's need was not to stop being nice, caring, or spontaneous but to better control these traits and balance them with others—assertiveness, firmness, and discipline—that he could use when needed. After the attempted coup, Paul realized what he needed to do and began to alter his personality. He continued to express the warm, friendly, caring traits that endeared him to others but he toned them down and worked on controlling them. He became more direct and forceful when necessary. As a result, he re-established his authority and the attempted coup ended. At the same time, realizing he needed help getting organized, he recruited some people who were better organized to help organize his office and set up a system to keep track of papers and tasks he needed to do.

Identifying Traits and Targeting Change

Aside from changing general personality traits, you can also target particular behaviors to change in certain situations. You may not change the inner you, but you can change the way you respond in a particular role. If you continue to use the same behaviors, it will eventually affect the inner you as well so you start to come into alignment with that inner role. It's much the same process that changes attitudes about anything. For example, if an individual who is biased is put in a situation where he is around people toward whom he or she originally has negative attitudes toward, in time those attitudes will generally diminish or disappear. Likewise, adopt the behaviors you want to express even if you feel uncomfortable about expressing them initially, and eventually you'll own those behaviors and make them part of you. If, for example, you have trouble being authoritative—you feel uncomfortable being in charge because you aren't sure people will follow your directions—visualize yourself being more powerful and authoritative and see yourself showing more leadership in your position.

Think of the difference between personality and behavior traits as the difference between the way you are and the way you act. The following exercise will help you identify the characteristics you want to eliminate and those you want to adopt.

Isolating the Personality or Behavior Traits to Change

For this exercise get a sheet of paper and pencil and divide the paper lengthwise into four columns. Head each one with the question you are asking. To begin, write down at the top of the first column and ask, *What behavioral or personality traits do I want to eliminate?* Be receptive and see what comes to you. Write down ideas or images as they come to mind. Don't try to judge whether you can get rid of that trait or not. Keep going until you have listed at least five traits or the images have started to slow down.

Then, at the top of the second column write down and ask, *What difficult situations have I encountered in the past few weeks?* Again, be receptive and just see what comes. As each scene appears, notice how you are acting and whether anything you are doing has been making this situation difficult for you. If so, this is probably a trait you will want to change. Write this trait in the second column. Keep going until you start to slow down.

Next, write down at the top of the third column and ask yourself, *What behavioral or personality traits do I want to acquire?* In some cases these traits may be the reverse of those you want to eliminate, while in other cases they may be entirely different ones. Whatever comes to you is fine. Just list them in the third column. Don't critique or evaluate the trait. And don't try to judge whether or not you can realistically acquire that trait. Again, keep going until you have listed at least five traits or have started to slow down.

Finally, write down at the top of the fourth column and ask, *What new situations would I like to be in where I am different from what I am now?* Again be receptive and see what comes. As each scene appears, notice what traits you have that are making the situation feel comfortable and natural. These may be behavior or personality traits you want to acquire but don't yet have. Write down in the fourth column any of these qualities that come up for you. Keep going until you start to slow down.

When you feel you have finished, you are ready to set priorities. Which traits do you want to eliminate or develop first? Look at the list of traits you want to eliminate. For each one, come up with the complementary or opposite trait you would like to acquire and list it in the third column (if you haven't already listed that trait in the third column). After you have listed this complementary trait or found it in the third column, cross out the trait you want to eliminate from the first column.

Now look down the list of all the traits in columns three and four and set priorities. To do so, rate each trait from zero to three, with zero being the lowest priority and three being the highest priority. Finally, look at the traits you have marked with the highest priority category. If you have more than one or two traits in this category, go through this list and rank them again until you have selected one or two traits that are the most important to you. If there are two, note which is most important to you. You have now established your priorities, so you can work first on developing the quality that is most important to you. If you would like to you can work on acquiring two qualities, but it's best not to work on more than two at a time. Once you feel certain you have made these a part of your behavioral repertoire, go on to the next trait on your list in order of priority. When you feel you've completed these and incorporated them into your collection, you may want to make a new list.

After you have identified the general and specific behavior and personality traits you want to change, you can work on changing your overall orientation, specific traits, or both, but don't try to change more than two or three things about yourself at a time. Remember, your global behavioral and personality traits represent your more general approach of relating to others and the world and reflect how you perceive information or make decisions. The particular behavioral traits are how you are likely to act, or habitual patterns of action, while the personality traits reflect predispositions to think, feel, believe, and have a certain type of attitude or orientation toward the world.

Mental Scripting:
How to See Yourself as You Want to Be

Now that you have identified the behavior and personality traits you want to eliminate or acquire, you can work on doing just that. A good way to do this is through mental scripting to create new patterns and approaches in your mind that you can then play out in real life. This technique to develop or eliminate personality traits is much like using a mental rehearsal technique to practice a particular skill or ability. In this case, however, you create a more detailed scenario in which you mentally play out a desired role again and again until you create a habit or pattern of action. As you repeatedly experience the action mentally, you reinforce the pattern in your mind. This, in turn, makes you feel more and more certain you can play the role and that confidence carries over into playing the scene in everyday life. You are a movie director again creating a scene for your movie; you create the setting where you play out your imagined script and possess the personality traits you desire.

For example, if you want to be more assertive and authoritative at work in order to advance your career, picture yourself as more assertive and authoritative in your present position and see others respond to you in a more cooperative, agreeable way acknowledging your desired leadership ability. You might see yourself giving instructions clearly and firmly, imagine others listening to you more seriously, and experience others coming to you for advice having recognized your authority and expertise. You might also project yourself into the future and see yourself expressing the desired leadership qualities in the position you want. You might see yourself in your new office feeling very comfortable and imagine yourself doing the tasks you want to do, such as giving instructions to your staff or attending a board meeting. In response, people defer to you and respect you in your new role. The following exercise will help you to create your own mental script.

Be Who You Want to Be

Decide which behavior or personality trait you want to work on changing or acquiring. As usual, get relaxed and close your eyes. Take a minute or two to focus on your breathing to get very calm and relaxed. Then, with the trait you want to change or acquire in mind, imagine a setting in which you want to express that trait. Tell yourself that you now have the trait you desire and see yourself expressing that trait in that setting in the present. You have been in the situation before, but now you are acting in this new way. See yourself doing this vividly. Notice the environment around you. Notice the colors, the people, the smells, and the objects around you. Experience yourself interacting and talking with others. As you do, remind yourself that you have this quality you want to have and you feel very comfortable, very natural, and very confident acting this new way. Experience this for a few minutes.

Now project yourself into the future to a situation you would like to be in where you have and utilize this trait. It might be a move, a promotion, or a new relationship. Whatever it is, tell yourself that you have the trait you want to have and see yourself expressing it in this future setting. You see this future scene clearly and vividly as if it is happening now. Again, notice the environment around you. Notice the colors, the people around you, the smells, and the objects. Experience yourself interacting and talking with others. As you do, remind yourself that you have this quality you want to have and you feel very comfortable, very natural, and very confident acting this new way. Again, experience this for a few minutes. When you feel ready, let go of the scene and let it fade. As it does you feel very good, very confident, and ready to put this new trait into practice.

Then, holding on to that feeling and enthusiasm to go out and do it, return to the room. Count backward from five to one, and as you do, you will come back. Five, four, becoming more and more alert; three, two, almost back; and one, you are back in the room.

Practicing Your Mental Script

Once you have created a mental script you like, practice applying it in the real world. Practice it a few minutes a day until you really feel the new trait become a part of you. Or at other times, replay this script in your mind to prepare yourself for the actual encounter. Then, should an appropriate situation arise, assert yourself and be firm or be warm and open as you saw yourself mentally. Whatever the scenario, remember the feeling of confidence you felt as you acted the way you wanted in your mental script.

Turning Your Mental Script into Everyday Reality

In the beginning you may have to pay extra attention to your mental script and keep reminding yourself that you are trying to change by substituting a new way of feeling and acting for an old one. You may need to replay parts of your script from time to time and pay careful attention to what you say and do in order to break old patterns and replace them with your new ones. Eventually, as you keep inserting your new script into the way you act, it will become a habit and after a while you won't need to use the script anymore. The new trait and your behavior pattern reflecting this trait will have become a part of you.

Chapter Nine

༄

Maximizing Your Skills and Abilities

Is there a skill you want to develop to help you at work such as improving your word processing skills, giving talks, or communicating better at meetings? Do you want to be more skilled in something you do at home such as becoming a great cook or learning how to fix things around the house? These GWYW techniques can help you improve in many areas. To develop any skill, use your power to create mental imagery to practice in your mind.

The power of the mind to affect performance has become widely recognized by researchers and trainers. Thousands of sports figures use mental imagery techniques to develop and perfect their skills and to help them win games and competitions. They mentally practice their sport to supplement their real practice, and before a big competition they psyche themselves up by visualizing themselves making the basket, hitting the home run, or winning the game. The power of these techniques is so great that specialists in peak performance have been working with coaches to train athletes in using imagery most effectively. Professionals in fields other than sports also use this technique. Hundreds of consultants and trainers have been showing business leaders and their employees how to use these techniques to improve productivity and boost morale. Even lawyers use this technique. For instance, after they prepare their written materials, many trial lawyers review exactly how they are going to present their argument in court in their mind. They visualize themselves speaking to the jury. They see themselves questioning and cross-examining witnesses. They go through all the different phases of the trial in their mind as the case moves on each day. Teachers, seminar leaders, salespeople, and countless others use this technique to develop and perfect their skills.

Once you get rid of any I can'ts standing in your way, you'll be free to develop your talents and skills. In all probability, you'll find you now can do many things you never dreamed possible and you can develop existing talents and skills to new levels of excellence.

GWYW Techniques to Improve Skills

The GWYW techniques can help to improve your skills in a number of ways. These include discovering and practicing new skills, overcoming fears that keep you from developing a skill, and increasing your income when you learn to perform a skill very well. Following are examples of individuals using each of these approaches to improve their skills.

Overcome Your Fear of New Activities

Suzanne used these techniques to discover how to become a better hostess at parties and events. She did this after she and her husband moved to a new town and she became a volunteer for a charity that she wanted to help out by hosting fundraising parties for the group. Using visualization techniques she imagined herself as a successful and outgoing hostess. As she saw herself in different roles as a hostess, from cooking up new recipes in the kitchen to meeting and greeting guests, she became increasingly aware that she really liked working with people to coordinate the event past just making invitation phone calls and she decided she might not only use this skill for volunteer events but might also make some additional money as an event planner. To become even better she continued her visualizations, so she imagined herself whipping up all kinds of recipes where she combined different foods in different ways and she imagined different activities she could plan for her guests. She saw herself leading a team of volunteers preparing the decorations and creating an exciting theme for the party. She also saw guests arriving, enjoying the party, and complimenting her on her unique new dishes. Then when it came time to actually plan and put the party together she knew exactly what to do. Visualization helped her feel fully prepared and full of confidence for the real thing. The result was a very enjoyable party, which was the first of many, and the beginning of a new part-time career as an event planner.

Overcoming Fears to Develop New Skills for a New Activity

In another case, Jack overcame his fear of water so he could learn how to swim. All his life Jack felt held back by this fear, and when he moved to a new house near a large lake he decided it was time to learn. He saw others go to the water to swim, be on water skis, or take out boats where knowing how to swim was expected and required for safety reasons. And he felt he was missing out by not being able to join in these activities with others. The prospect of swimming frightened him, although he realized he had to do it. He began taking steps to overcome his fears using both actual practice and GWYW techniques. To gain practice, he joined a swimming class where he practiced going farther and farther into the lake to get over his fear. At the same time, he spent a few minutes each day visualizing himself fearlessly going into the water. He imagined going in deeper and deeper, and then gradually lying down in the water where he experienced images of both humans and animals, such as dolphins and fish, effortlessly propelling themselves through the water. At the same time he imagined himself being calm, confident, and completely relaxed and comfortable. He then imagined himself easily swimming like the dolphins, fish, and expert swimmers.

The result was that a few weeks later he was able to swim quickly and confidently as he joined others at the lake to swim and enjoy water sports. He had developed a belief from his practice that he could do it. When he began swimming in the lake outside of the swimming class he felt like he could almost go automatically because he had practiced so many times in his mind. As a result, when he actually did what he had imagined he knew exactly what to do and had no fear doing it. He had acquired that sense of knowing and assurance that comes from practice—even if much of that practice was in his mind.

Earn More through Improved Performance

Better performance can lead to increased income, as one salesman found when he used visualization to become better at his job. Before that, Jerry had tried various sales jobs after leaving college and eventually went through a real estate program and sold real estate for a large company. But he was disappointed by his lackluster performance compared to the other salespeople. He was only making a few sales a month and experiencing a 95 percent rejection rate, whereas some of the company's top performers were averaging six or seven sales a month and closing about 10–15 percent of the people they worked with. Then, at a sales meeting, Jerry heard a speaker talk about the power of creative visualization and tried it out by spending fifteen minutes each day before he went to bed visualizing himself giving a sales pitch to his prospects. He saw himself taking them to a house, giving them an enthusiastic buildup on the way, and listening to what they wanted. He also imagined arriving at the house, showing the prospects around, and telling them about the benefits they would find especially appealing.

Within a few days Jerry noticed a powerful effect. He found he gave his sales talk about the homes more convincingly, and seemed to know exactly what to say and when because he had already practiced in his mind. Also, he felt more enthusiastic as he spoke, just as he had when he practiced. In turn, his prospects were more responsive. They appeared to be more reassured by what he said, felt he was more knowledgeable, and trusted his claims more, and their more favorable attitude showed in his sales.

Mental Scripts to Plan and Rehearse

The key to increasing your skills with these GWYW techniques is rehearsing what you want in your mind. By doing so, you reinforce what you have learned through physical practice since the mind doesn't clearly distinguish between what you do in reality and what you do mentally. The result is that you can cut down on actual practice time and speed up the time you need to improve. Furthermore, by working with the skill you want to acquire in your mind, you can see yourself performing it perfectly, which provides an ideal model you can strive to achieve when you perform the activity for real. Using the ideal model is crucial for your success since you need to see yourself doing the skill perfectly to attain this goal. Otherwise, if you make mistakes in your mental practice, you'll make the same mistakes in the real world. So, to improve your singing skills see yourself singing every note correctly; to improve your sales ability, see yourself making a perfect presentation, asking the right questions, and closing each sale. If a mistake should appear as you visualize, simply imagine yourself quickly correcting it. You want to create an image of perfection to influence what you do in real life.

Mental imaging techniques work because they give you the ability to plan what you want to do and practice doing it. In addition, as you actively see yourself performing well through practice, you reinforce what you have learned from physically performing that act or learning that skill. By doing so, you gain the confidence that comes from practice. If you can actually practice, that would be even better. But even if you just rehearse in your mind, you are practicing and your mind creates a mental script so real that when it comes time for the real thing you can use your mental script as a guide.

This mental scripting approach is so powerful because when you perform well mentally, the mind sets up an effective pattern (like a habit), which in creating mental images that lay down traces in the brain cells, transfers over into the real performance. You see yourself performing something perfectly that, in turn, provides an ideal model you can strive toward when you are actually doing it. Practicing in your mind also reduces the amount of actual practice time needed, and therefore, helps you improve more quickly. Then, too, as you visualize going through the experience, you learn what you need to add or change to improve your performance.

I use these techniques regularly while preparing for talks and presentations. I mentally go through all the steps a few times to decide what materials I am going to use in a presentation and how I am going to use them. Then I mentally rehearse the broad outlines of my talk, and if I need to make any changes or additions to what I say or how I say it, this practice gives me the chance to make them. By the time I actually give the talk, everything I need to do it well is in place and I feel confident I can do it.

Similarly you can use visualization to build your skills, perhaps starting off by deciding what you want to practice. For instance, I begin by using a series of visualizations to ask myself what I need to do and then prepare accordingly. If it's a seminar, for example, I create an outline and workbook and then imagine myself giving the talk. I see myself up on the platform. Using the outline I go through each topic in my mind, making appropriate changes and additions when necessary. When the time comes to give my talk I am confident I can do it. I know in my mind what I can do, and when the seminar begins I step out on the stage and it's as if I had done it many times before. Once I start speaking, everything seems to fall right into place just as I had imagined it. The ideas and words are right there when I need them and I zip along following my outline. When it comes time for audience participation, the audience, too, slips right into place. It all works because I go over everything in advance in my mind's eye. As a result I know what I am going to do and have the confidence to do it.

The I can approach opens the door and the mental script technique helps you through it.

The Keys to an Effective Mental Rehearsal

To use the mental rehearsal technique successfully, keep the following key points in mind:

Select a Method You Have Learned to Do or Have Seen Someone Else Use and Visualize This in Your Mind

For instance, if you have just learned some basic procedures for using a mobile app, see yourself going through these procedures in your mind. Or if you have seen someone give an impressive speech, imagine yourself giving a talk using the same approach as this speaker.

Visualize a New Method in Your Mind—See Yourself Doing it Right

This image in your mind will eventually translate into reality. Create an ideal model to guide your performance. Imagine doing whatever you are doing flawlessly and effectively since the image in your mind is what will gradually translate itself into reality. If you make mistakes in your mental practice, you'll make the same mistakes in the real world. If you imagine yourself performing perfectly, you may not perform perfectly in the real world but you'll perform more closely to perfection. Whatever skill you choose to develop, imagine that you know exactly what to do. For example, to improve your typing skills see yourself hitting every key correctly and quickly. To be a better speaker, see yourself making the perfect presentation.

Quickly Correct Any Mistakes

As you visualize, if you make a mistake imagine yourself quickly correcting it. For example, if you are imagining a job interview and say the wrong thing, back up to what you were doing before you made the error and give your answer again.

Imagine Practicing New Skills

Make your imagination as intense and vivid as possible; make the image as detailed and real as possible. The more real you make the mental experience, the more powerful it will be in influencing what happens when you actually do it. So don't just visualize yourself using the desired skills effectively, but hear, feel, smell, and otherwise sense the environment. Clearly visualize the setting. See yourself or others dressed appropriately to practice that skill; notice anyone else in the environment. Pay attention to what others are doing. Are they responding to you, listening closely, and enjoying your comments?

Repeat This Visualization Again and Again

This will give it more power. Like an athlete or performer, you have to practice in your mind just as in life. Repeat your visualization at least once a day, or more if needed. By doing so it becomes automatic, a habit. If necessary, you can replay this guiding imagery in your mind at any time.

Invest the Image with the Feeling of Becoming More Skilled, Confident, and Assured

You want to invest the image with these feelings because they will stay with you when you return to normal consciousness and will help you perform better in real life. When you feel good about what you are doing, you will enjoy doing it and will do it better. So as you practice feel yourself becoming more skilled, confident, and assured, and this feeling will carry over into real time and help you perform better. When you return to normal consciousness, carry this feeling of success and confidence with you.

Avoid Second-Guessing Yourself

After you have successfully visualized what you want, allow yourself to feel a sense of completion. Don't question whether the process works or ask, *Can I really do this?* Such questions will undermine what you have done. You have to truly believe that mental imaging will work for it to do so. Should questions about the process arise, push them away. Keep reinforcing your self-confidence and assure yourself that you can do it. That, too, will help you do it.

Find a Good Role Model

Even if you already have some experience with a skill you want to develop, a good role model can give you an ideal to strive toward in your mental practicing. Ideally, observe the person in action. Then imagine yourself in this person's place, reenacting as closely as possible what this person did so well. For instance, if you have seen someone give an impressive speech, imagine yourself giving a talk using the same approach. If you have met someone who is especially adept in meeting and talking to people, pay attention to what they do and mentally practice these methods.

Sample Visualizations

The following visualizations will give you some ideas of how to use the process. They can be adapted to the skill you want to acquire or improve on since the particular skills desired and current level of training will vary for each person. You can also use the principles underlying these examples to create your own visualizations for the skill you want to acquire.

Imagine You Possess the Skill You Want to Acquire

To begin, close your eyes and get relaxed. Focus on your breathing for a minute or two to calm down. Now ask yourself what skill, talent, or ability you want to acquire. Let a word or picture of this skill come into your mind. Then picture someone performing that skill very well. It could be a person you know or even someone well-known. It can be anyone. Just watch the person in action.

Watch the person closely. They seem to be completely at ease. They are doing it very well. Notice how they move. Notice their gestures. Notice that they feel very confident and assured. They have a lot of enthusiasm. They really like what they are doing and are totally into doing it. Maybe there are others watching, too, and admiring what they are doing. Continue to watch for a while, really getting a sense of what they are doing so you see what to do yourself.

Now, after you have watched for a while, go over to the person you have been watching. Explain how much you have admired what they have done and ask them to be your teacher. Explain how much you really want to learn to do this yourself and listen to the person's answers. If the person says no, ask again. If the answer is still no perhaps you aren't quite ready to learn this skill or to learn from this teacher. Ask why.

If the answer is yes, see yourself getting ready to learn this skill and see your teacher nearby watching and ready to help. Then, recalling how you saw your teacher do it, imagine yourself doing it. If you're not sure of something you can always turn to your teacher to ask for help. Now spend a few minutes practicing this skill as your teacher watches. Notice how you move as you do it. Notice how you are feeling very confident and assured that you will do well. Also, you have lots of enthusiasm. You really like what you are doing and feel totally absorbed.

When you feel ready, stop practicing and thank your teacher for helping, knowing you can always call on them to help again. Then let this image go, return to the room, and open your eyes feeling very good and confident in your new abilities.

Practice a Skill or Talent You Want to Develop

To begin, close your eyes and get relaxed. Focus on your breathing for a minute or two to calm down. Ask yourself what skill, talent, or ability you want to further develop. Then see yourself ready to perform this skill with whatever equipment you will need to do this. If you wish, invite your teacher to come and observe and make comments and suggestions.

Now, whatever the skill is, see yourself doing it. Notice that you feel comfortable and very much at ease. Experience yourself performing this skill well, and as you do, notice how you are moving. You are moving easily. You feel competent and confident. Should you make a mistake, you can quickly correct it; or if your teacher is there, ask them how to correct it. Or you can turn and see someone near you practicing the same skill and doing it perfectly. You can copy what this person is doing so you know exactly what to do. If you wish, you can have others around who are just watching, praising, and cheering you.

Take a few minutes to continue to practice, doing it well and feeling self-assured and powerful. You know you are very good and are getting even better as you practice. Then, when you feel ready, finish practicing and if you have had any help, thank whoever helped. If others have been watching, thank them for their support. Then let the image go, return to the room, and open your eyes feeling good and confident that you are getting better and better in your abilities.

Improve Your Speaking Ability in a Group

To begin, again close your eyes and relax. Now see yourself in your office or in a quiet place at work. You have some time to prepare for an upcoming group meeting and you go over what you are going to say in your mind. See yourself thinking of the key points you want to make. Imagine how you are going to say them and which points you will make first.

Then rehearse these ideas in your mind. Say them again and again to yourself until you feel certain of what you want to say and how to say it. Now, feeling sure of yourself, imagine you are with that group. You enter the room feeling very confident about what you are going to say. Then you present your arguments or comments. You do so forcefully and authoritatively, and you notice that the others are listening closely to what you say. When you are finished, they agree with you.

As the conversation continues, you make additional points from time to time, and again, you know exactly when to say what you need to say and you phrase it exactly the right way. In turn, the other group members highly value your ideas and show their approval by listening closely and praising what you say.

Continue to practice in your mind's eye for a few minutes and notice your sureness and control. Notice how much your speaking ability has improved and how much surer of yourself you are. Slowly come back to the room and open your eyes. This feeling will stay with you when you return to normal consciousness and you will notice an immediate improvement the next time you speak in a group or give a presentation.

Improve Your Reading Ability

To begin, close your eyes and relax. Picture yourself in front of a physical book or reading on your computer or mobile device. Sit down at it and open the book to a page, ready to start reading. You feel very comfortable. Scan your eyes over the document.

Now, place your first two fingers at the beginning of the document and walk them along the document. Follow the words under your fingers with your eyes. Then as you turn the pages or flip from page to page in the document, move your fingers more quickly down the page, and again follow your fingers with your eyes. Gradually, quicken the pace so you can still comprehend the meaning of what you are reading, although you don't have to mentally mouth or think each word. This is actually a technique used in a rapid reading class to increase reading speed while maintaining comprehension.

Now you will add in the power of your mind to imagine you are doing this. Just see the image of the book you have been reading in your mind and imagine your fingers walking through the text as you read, and as in the real experience, speed up the movement of your fingers in your mind while you still understand what you are reading. Continue doing this process for a few minutes, and when you find a top speed you are comfortable with, stay at that speed and practice on a series of pages. Later you can up the speed and find a new plateau on which to practice. Finally, when you actually sit down with a book or with something to read on your computer or mobile device, you will find you can read faster with increased accuracy whether you use your real fingers or imagine your fingers are walking across the page.

Creating Your Own Skills Visualizations

You can also use the formats I have described to create your own skills visualizations. These exercises are just models you can use to develop new skills or practice others you want to further develop. Such skills and abilities can run the gamut from job or hobby skills to social skills. You can insert whatever skill you want to develop into these scenarios or create your own visualizations. It can be anything from an elaborate setting to practice your skills to just seeing yourself practicing in your mind's eye. Simply decide what skill you want to develop, create a mental scenario where you are in a setting that you are comfortably using that skill, and see yourself doing it perfectly. For the visualization to be most effective make the image and experience as vivid and intense as possible so that it feels very real. It's important to notice any mistakes as you practice and to correct them immediately so you don't carry the errors over into your performance.

After you have practiced several times you will immediately begin seeing the results in your improved performance. Continue doing the visualization until you have acquired the facility you want with the particular skill. Once you attain that level, if you perform the skill regularly your everyday habit reflexes will take over. Once you attain this automatic performance level, you'll be able to perform the skill automatically and effectively and won't need to practice mentally on a regular basis. Then from time to time, to polish your abilities, go over your skill in your mind. If you expect to use these skills for a particularly critical occasion, such as a big presentation to a client or a keynote speech to a business group, mentally review so that you feel completely prepared and psyched up to put on your best possible performance.

Should you attain a desired level and want to improve even more, simply bring up the image of your ideal accomplishment in your mind. For example, if you want to use that skill even more quickly, increase the speed in your visualization and practice at that new speed until you feel comfortable at this new plateau. Or to get even better, such as perfecting your ability to cook a better soufflé or sing with more style and passion, choose an even more skilled teacher as your model and practice to achieve that level. Just as in everyday life you want to keep improving, so likewise you need to improve the models you use to practice in your mind.

Chapter Ten

❧

Unleash Your Creativity and Innovation

Your ability to be creative can be an essential component of getting what you want since your creativity helps you adapt to change, as well as come up with new productive ideas—from different strategies for getting what you want to coming up with new products and services you can use to increasing your income or starting a new career or company.

Your inner creativity can help you be more efficient and productive, create new useful and profitable products or businesses, design better policies and procedures so offices or groups can function, and provide more and better leadership and direction. It can also help you reshape yourself and what you do to open doors to new opportunities. It can help you feel more power and self-confidence so you can do more, make life more interesting and exciting for you and others in your life, and much more. You imagine it and you can create whatever your imagination comes up with. The focus of this chapter is on increasing your creative abilities, from using them to make changes to coming up with new ideas.

Using Your Creativity to Respond to Change

Creativity is an essential part of human nature—a kind of evolutionary key—that has enabled humans to thrive. Our environment is always changing and our creativity helps us respond to or influence that change. Creativity allows us to constantly remake ourselves and remodel our behavior to best fit the new conditions or sometimes shape the new conditions. Today's technological revolution is a good example. It has transformed the way many of us live and work, and it has changed life's pace. Most people have had to adapt to these changes to one degree or another.

There is often great resistance to change because people are afraid of where it will lead. They fear it may be dangerous—and sometimes change can be—particularly if it is unanticipated or out of control. But when you are receptive and view change in a positive and productive way, you discover how many possibilities it offers and how much you can gain from change. How receptive are you? There are some key questions to ask yourself about how good you are at recognizing or anticipating changes in your life. Are there major changes you are experiencing now or that you anticipate in the near future? Are there any things you should change in what you are doing?

You can use the following exercise to note changes and what you might do to respond.

Recognizing and Responding to Change

Get comfortable and relaxed. Then ask yourself the following questions, wait and listen for the answers, and write them down.

- What major changes have recently occurred in my life? In my work? In my relationships?
- What have I done to respond to them?

- How well do I feel I responded? (Rate your responses from zero to five.)

- What should I do now, if anything, to respond to these changes?

- What major changes do I anticipate occurring in the next three to six months that will affect me? In my work? In my relationships?

- What can I do to respond to these changes?

- What major changes do I anticipate occurring in the next six months to a year that will affect me? In my work? In my relationships?

- What can I do to respond to these changes?

After you have finished answering your questions, let go and return to your normal state. Review your answers and consider which of these responses you want to implement now.

Creative Repackaging: How to Present the New You

Reviewing the changes that have affected or will affect you and how you can change may lead you to realize your need to present yourself in new ways to adjust to new times. In turn, changing yourself can help you convince others you can do something new or different. By presenting yourself in a new way, you change how people view you and their perceptions of what you can do. It signifies that you are ready and able to respond to change.

This is what happened to Bill, a lawyer specializing in immigration. He had done very well, but after twelve years doing immigration law he felt burned out. Though immigration had become a major news topic and his background was impressive, it was specialized, and those hiring in related fields couldn't see past his highly developed, but specialized, skills in helping immigrants—a narrow focus made even more salient by immigration being a hot button subject in the news. For Bill, creativity meant thinking of new ways to present himself. He looked at the skills he used in being a successful immigration lawyer and the results he had achieved in using those skills rather than at the particular tasks he had done. As a result, he repackaged himself as a problem solver and operational development specialist. He stopped using the term lawyer or attorney to describe himself, despite working in this capacity for more than twelve years. Instead, by creatively repackaging himself he not only saw himself in a new way, but also created a new prism through which prospective employers could regard him. As a result, within a few weeks he found a new job helping managers troubleshoot and resolve problems in their organizations.

The Three Keys to Creativity

While creativity is often thought of in terms of results, such as how you decide to change or the new ideas you come up with, these results are only the end product. Being creative is also a process of responding in new ways. It can be harnessed to do everything from creating different forms of artistic expression to reshaping yourself, your relationships, your work environment, and society as a whole. Underlying this creativity is a readiness to respond, a willingness to try, openness to new things, and a lack of fear of change. When you combine these qualities with an awareness of what needs fixing or changing, you can apply these techniques to come up with new ideas for just about anything. The three basic elements that facilitate the creativity process are:

1) The ability to perceive and think in innovative ways. An approach that helps you come up with new ideas using techniques such as brainstorming and intuition to envision alternatives.

2) An openness to alternative approaches so you're willing to accept new ideas and act on them.

3) The insight to identify areas in which creative responses are needed giving you the ability to perceive which changes are necessary or desirable and which aren't.

These three elements represent a creative approach to life that can be applied to anything. If you learn to incorporate a creative approach to whatever you do, you can call on your creative force at any time and for a variety of purposes. Creativity becomes part of who you are, a natural way of being, so you are always ready to use it.

Overcoming Blocks to Creativity

Sometimes creativity can be blocked because of a fear of new ideas or of making changes. This fear can also prevent you from recognizing where a new idea or a change is needed or from jumping on a new opportunity due to a fear of the risk or downside of doing so. Certainly there are times it is prudent to be cautious and to make sure the opportunity is a valid one, but other times too much due diligence can hold you back when all other signs are telling you to go. For each new invention, you can find people who were happy with the old idea, resisted the new, and were subsequently left behind—the silent movie producers who rejected the coming of sound, decision makers at Hewlett-Packard who didn't see any sense in the personal computer idea of employees who left and founded Apple, or the resistance of IBM executives to the software system ideas of Ross Perot who made billions from them. At one time company owners even expressed a resistance to getting telephones because they had messenger boys on bikes to deliver their messages.

Fear and resistance in daily life can be roadblocks as well. The following exercises will help you to identify and overcome any fears and resistances you might have. They are designed to help you look within to discover either a general nay-saying attitude or a specific fear about a particular situation that is holding you back. The first exercise is concerned with your attitude, and the second is intended to help with a particular fear or situation.

Overcoming a Negative Attitude

Get comfortable and relaxed, as usual. Close your eyes. Focus on your breathing for a minute or so until you feel very centered and relaxed. Now take a mental journey to wherever you want to go to get inner information—a quiet, calm place or a room where you can meet your inner expert—and ask yourself a series of questions to see if you are afraid of or resistant to new things or to some specific things. As you ask each question, don't try to answer it with your conscious mind. Instead, just listen or observe and wait for the answer to come to you.

Ask this question first and listen to the answer, *How do I feel about new ideas? Do I like things that are new or different?*

Next, ask and listen again. *How do I usually react when I experience something new and different?* Ask to see a few examples; they can be situations at work or in your personal life. Take a few minutes to look at these situations. Notice what comes up. Have you usually been receptive? If you have been receptive, compliment yourself for being open and remind yourself that you will continue to be so in the future. Then gradually bring yourself back to normal consciousness and return to the room.

If you are normally not receptive, ask yourself *Why am I resistant to new ideas or changes? What fears are standing in the way? Why am I apt to say no? Why am I holding back from being open to change?* Notice the answers.

Now, if you feel ready to rid yourself of these fears imagine that you are collecting these fears together. Imagine that each of these fears is an object and you are picking them up one by one to get rid of them. You can burn them, bury them, throw them in the river, or bomb them. However you want to do it, see these fears disappearing. As each one disappears, feel yourself getting freer and freer. You feel more open and receptive, more ready to see new ideas without criticizing, prejudging, or thinking them wrong in advance. In fact, you are now eager to learn about new ideas and try them out. Your fear of doing so is gone and you feel ready to do and discover new things.

Holding that feeling of interest and excitement, tell yourself, *In the future I will be more open and receptive. I will be more ready to hear about and act on new things. If I feel myself resisting and holding back, I will tell myself "No. Don't say no. Be open. Be ready to wait and see."*

Repeat this reminder to yourself several times while feeling this sense of interest and excitement. Then, let go of this experience, leave the place you have gone to get information, and return to your everyday consciousness.

Overcoming a Fear

As usual, get comfortable and relaxed. Close your eyes, and focus on your breathing for a minute or so until you feel very centered and relaxed.

Now take a mental journey wherever you want to get inner information—a quiet, calm place or a room where you can meet your inner expert—and ask yourself a series of questions to see if you are afraid of or resistant to a specific new idea or situation. As you ask each question, don't try to consciously answer it. Instead, listen or observe and wait for the answer to come to you.

Ask yourself the following question and listen to the answer. *Why do I fear this new idea or change or particular situation (describe it)? What do I see holding me back?* Then listen to the answer. Are you afraid of someone? Is it something you have to do that bothers you? Are you afraid of being wrong? Do you fear coming up with ideas that aren't good? Reflect on what comes to you. If you are ready to get rid of these fears, imagine that you are collecting them. Imagine that each of these fears is like an object or painting and you are picking them up one by one to get rid of them. You can burn them, bury them, throw them in the river, or bomb them. However you want to do it, see these fears disappearing. As each one disappears, you feel freer and freer. You feel more open and receptive. You are more ready to approach this situation in a new way. You are ready to think of new ideas without criticizing, prejudging, or thinking them wrong in advance. You are now eager to tackle this idea or situation. Your fear of doing so is gone.

Holding that feeling of interest and excitement, tell yourself, *I am ready and eager to deal with this situation now. I will be more ready to hear about and act on these new ideas. If I feel myself beginning to resist or hold back, I will tell myself,* "No. Don't say no. Be open. Be ready to consider and try out this new idea or situation. There's nothing to be concerned about or afraid of. I'll think of the possibilities and know it will be possible. I'll say yes to these possibilities. I'll say yes to these possibilities."

Repeat this reminder several times while feeling this sense of interest and excitement. Then let go of this experience and return to your everyday consciousness.

Identifying What Needs Changing

In what areas do you need new ideas? What would you like to change? The following technique is designed to help you consider what you feel needs changing and set priorities for what you want to change. Then you can brainstorm or use your intuition to seek new ideas and help you select among alternatives. Have a paper and pencil ready to list the areas where new ideas or changes are needed.

To begin, get comfortable and relaxed. Close your eyes. Focus on your breathing to get into this centered state. Now take a mental journey to wherever you want to go to get inner information just as the previous techniques have described. Then ask yourself, *What new things or changes would I like to see in my life?* List whatever comes.

If you are interested in making changes in a particular area, such as at work, at home, or in a certain relationship, ask about that. *What new things or changes would I like to see in _____?* Again, list whatever comes.

Finally ask, *Are there any other new things or changes I would like to make?* Again list whatever comes. After you've listed all you can think of, let go of the experience and return to your everyday consciousness. Review the list you have created and rate the areas on a rating system of zero to three, with zero being no interest and three being of high interest on which you want to focus first. If there are more than a few high-priority areas, go back to those and rate your priorities within this group. Once you have set your priorities, you can focus on applying idea-generating techniques to these areas.

Using Your Creativity to Generate Ideas

Just like any skill, the ability to be creative—the ability to come up with new ideas, do things differently, think of alternative approaches, and apply them effectively—can be developed through practice. It's like any skill on a continuum, from having little to an average amount to a great deal of creativity, and through practice you can increase where you fall on this continuum. (Or alternatively, if you don't use your creative abilities, you can become rusty though you can refresh your skills to further develop them at any time.) So just as you can get better at writing, speaking, or anything else by doing it, so too can you become more creative by taking the time to work on coming up with and using new ideas. The more you do it, the easier it gets since you are in effect exercising your creative muscle and getting more in touch with the intuitive idea-generating part of your mind. Whatever the arena, you will find you have more ideas.

As being creative effectively is a process, rather than the end product of being creative, these techniques focus on helping you adopt the attitudes you need to be more creative. Then you can apply this outlook to any area you choose to express your creativity, ranging from organizing your office to coming up with ideas for new products, programs, or organizations. The following methods are particularly valuable in the workplace, but you can easily adapt them to come up with ideas in all areas of your life. The exercises will help you develop your creative abilities generally as well as provide some techniques you can apply in everyday work and personal situations. You can use any of these techniques alone or try brainstorming with a friend or in a group. Following are three key ways of being creative that you can apply to become more creative in the workplace or in your personal life.

1. Seeing New Uses for Things.

A perfect example of this is how the extremely successful Post-it notes were developed. Someone came up with the wrong glue formula and it wasn't strong enough, but someone else thought of a new way to use that glue for temporary attachments and it turned into a million-dollar business.

2. Use New Methods and Materials to Change What Already Exists.

The famous dictum "necessity is the mother of invention" can be especially appropriate. For instance, suppose you are following a recipe for a dinner party and suddenly discover that one or more items in the recipe are missing, or you don't have enough of them, and there is no time to get to the supermarket to buy them. This might be a time to find an alternative recipe you invent yourself from other items in your kitchen cabinet, or divide what you have from the original recipe into smaller dishes and create a new dish of your own with the items you have on hand.

3. Making Changes in What Already Exists or Combining What Exists in New Ways.

Frequently such change is vital to keep people stimulated and excited at work or to keep a series of regular parties from feeling like the same old, same old attitude. You want to add variety to spice up the usual activities. For example, people can often get bored if they have to do the same things every day or if a series of events with the same crowd feature the same activities. People want something new to add excitement to their lives. Otherwise, they can get stale working with the same team of people or going to a party with the same crowd as usual. But if an employer juggles tasks and people around or a party host comes up with new foods to try, new music, or new activities, this can get people energized and enthusiastic again.

The more you develop your abilities in these areas, the more creative you become and the more you can direct your creativity to be more effective in your work or personal life. The following exercises are designed to help you mobilize these creative processes so you can apply them as you wish. The examples given are merely illustrative. There are so many ways to apply your creativity depending on your goal. The key point is that once you increase your creativity, you can apply it to be more innovative in anything you want to do.

Method 1: See New Uses for Things; Finding New Ways to Use What You Have

This method will get you thinking about new uses for things. You begin by imagining new uses for familiar items to get your creative juices flowing. Then you apply the process to a specific situation, such as at work or at home, where you really do want to discover some new uses for things. Seeing new uses for things is the essence of innovation, and there are countless benefits. You can cut down your costs by finding new uses for a tool or equipment in your house so you don't have to buy something else. You can reduce expenses by using some items you already have for other purposes. You can use something designed for another use as a tool you don't have, such as using a spoon handle to pry open a lid when you don't have a can opener. You can expand the market for a product you are selling online by thinking of different ways that other groups can use it, such as turning decorated placemats into something that can be an attractive wall piece as well. In fact, some entrepreneurs have made millions by discovering a novel and popular use for something, such as turning a simple stone into a bestselling novelty by calling it a Pet Rock. If you have something and can think of new ways to use it, you can save money, increase its value to yourself and others, use it as a substitute for something else, or pitch it to a new market and earn money from your idea.

The first exercise is a kind of warm-up, while the second provides a more in-depth use of this process.

What's New?

See how many new and unusual uses you can create for familiar things. The idea is to start with something familiar and then see how many ways you can change and adapt it for new purposes. Try this alone or brainstorm with a friend or associate.

Begin by getting some paper and a pencil and writing down the names of some familiar objects. Perhaps look around your office or house and jot down the objects you see. Now, for each object write down as many uses as you can, making them as novel as possible. Feel free to change the size, shape, or color of the object as well, or combine two or more objects and think up uses for them together. For example, what can you do with a paper clip? A ruler? A pair of scissors? A lamp? What can you do with a piece of paper and a chair? A newspaper and a cup? A stapler and a picture hook? Now you take that away.

When you feel warmed up, think about any specific situations in your life where you might want to apply this technique. For example, if you have young kids you might imagine the way some common objects around your house might be turned into fun toys. If you are selling a new product online or in a store, think of all the possible uses for it or of all the ways you might advertise it. Or, if you are part of a work group or social group, think of all the things the group can do besides what it is doing now. The exercise is divided into two parts that will help to get your ideas flowing and help you to apply the process in a real situation.

Part 1: The Practice Warm Up

To get your creative juices flowing choose the first common objects that come to mind: things in your office, home, on the street, or natural objects. Make a list of these objects and pick five to ten you want to work on. For each of these objects, list as many ways as you can think of to use it. What are all the things you can do with a glass? A lightbulb? A box? A leaf? A piece of paper and a mirror? Feel free to come up with novel, unusual, even outrageous uses. Feel free to change the object's size, shape, or color or to use two or more objects together in new ways.

Part 2: Applying the Process

When you feel warmed-up, think of something at work or in your personal life to which you want to apply this technique. For example, you might think of new uses for products in your product line, new ways to use your computer or mobile device, new activities your work group or social group can do, or new no-cost activities you can do at home with your family. Now think about other ways or things to which you might apply this technique. Later, you can actually do so.

Method 2: Finding New Methods, Materials, or Paths to Attain a Goal

There are many paths to any goal—whether it's a personal goal such as taking a trip, a career goal such as finding a new job, or an accomplishment such as writing a song or publishing a book. Sometimes a clear path leads to your goal or you already have what you need to get there. At other times the path isn't clear, you're missing something, or you think you lack what you need to get there. That's when your creativity can help you find an alternate method, develop the skills, or discover the needed resources to reach your goal. You may already have these resources available but just don't know it. As in a maze, different approaches can be used to create the path to your goal. Additionally, when you have a goal, you need to believe you can reach it. By accessing your creativity you'll come up with a variety of approaches, choose the one approach or ones you want to try and believe you can do it. And you can!

For example, say you want to date someone you met at a party, but your initial meeting was very brief so you didn't have a chance to talk and get to know each other. Perhaps you could find out this person's interests or memberships—perhaps with the help of a friend or the party host—and you turn up at one of these activities and start talking there. Or suppose you want to be hired for a particular job or project and you are sure you can do it. But the requirements ask for some credentials or experience you don't have. If you want the assignment badly enough, come up with alternate ways to get it such as showing the people doing the hiring that this credential isn't necessary and you can do a better job than anyone else.

How do you come up with these creative approaches? That's where your GWYW powers come in to tap your creativity so you can come up with different ideas and choose the best ones to put into practice; and then they can help you in coming up with the steps to execute the plan. For instance, to meet the man or woman of your dreams at an activity where you can show you have a common interest, you might need to develop some knowledge about that activity, plan a few things to say to get the conversation going, and arrange to go to an event where this person will be. Or suppose you are trying for a job where you don't have the specific credentials required. You might need to assemble a personal portfolio on your background that includes some powerful testimonial or reference letters from important people. Then when you have the interview, you might imagine what you will say in advance so you can act with confidence and show your expertise as if you already have the job and no one else could be as good as you.

For example, Millie found her husband this way after moving to a new city. She saw him across the room at a party but didn't have a chance to talk to him there. She asked the friend who brought her there about him and learned he was an avid sailor. As a result, she joined the local yacht club where he was a member, took some sailing lessons, and just happened to bump into him at a monthly networking event for club members. Then she kicked off the conversation by talking about some recent sailing events in the news and segued into asking him about his own participation in sailing competitions. They later got together for dinner to talk more. One thing led to another as she realized she wanted to get serious with this man and finally realized her dream of marrying him.

The process of finding new methods or materials to attain exactly what you want can work with anything. The key is to think you can do it, whatever it is, and then determine what you need to do to accomplish it. You may be able to use what you already have on hand, although perhaps you must use it in a new way; or perhaps you need to get other resources and come up with creative ways to get them. For instance, suppose you have to put up some pictures in the office and forgot your hammer. Maybe something else will work—say the bottom of a hole puncher, a board under the coffee maker, or the heel of your shoe. In fact, if you come up with an invention to fulfill a major need, such as an attractively decorated shoulder holder for a smartphone, you might find a company may want to buy your invention or try making it yourself as a side venture.

The following techniques will help you loosen up your thinking processes so you are better able to create new approaches to achieve your goals.

New Look

As a kind of brain training exercise to limber up your ability to think quickly, see how many ways you can think of to fill a need. Brainstorm with a friend or associate if you wish. First, on a sheet of paper make a short list of some activities you'd like to see handled another way, such as traveling downtown to go shopping, organizing the office staff, or keeping burglars away from your house. Next, look at each activity individually and write down as many new approaches as you can, making them as novel as possible. Imagine you have unlimited resources to create solutions and let your ideas come as quickly as possible. Later, you can evaluate these ideas and choose the ones you can use.

Finding New Paths to a Chosen Goal

The following exercise will help you focus on finding new paths to a chosen goal. These paths can be new strategies and procedures or new materials and resources—whatever is needed to get there. In this exercise, you start with a goal you want to achieve or a need you want to satisfy. Then see how many ways you can achieve it. Have some paper and pencil handy to write down ideas.

Think of any goal or need. It can be something work-related or personal. Then brainstorm all the ways you can get there. Write them down. Consider both the different methods and resources you will need to get there. When you've come up with all the ideas you can, review them and choose those you can actually implement.

Method 3: New Ways to Change What Already Exists or Combining What Exists in New Ways

Making something different or better is a key benefit of creativity and innovation, and it's the engine of progress and change that has fueled modern technology and generated the race to produce better, state-of-the-art equipment. Change is the basis of technological and social progress—making changes in the way things are and combining what exists in new ways. Just think of the many positive words in our language that express the high value we place on the benefits of creative change: new, better, improved, faster, more efficient, more effective, cheaper, more attractive, more exciting … you can undoubtedly continue the list yourself. The point is that altering different elements or making new connections and combinations can change almost anything. Likewise, you can use this approach to improve your own life.

For example, use your creativity to reorganize your house or change the decor. Perhaps add new items like wall hangings or plants to make your home look more attractive or friendly so people feel more comfortable and receptive when they talk to you. Or if you're on a tight budget, turn old material into a brand-new piece of furniture. By applying a little change and innovation, and perhaps combining some things you already have in new ways, you can make something better, more attractive, or usable for something and have fun trying out different possibilities.

To make the most of this process, however, you must be receptive to innovation and enthusiastic about the potential of everything to change. In other words, you must both accept change and be ready to initiate it as the situation requires, and you'll find the results pay off for you in very attractive ways, such as a more appealing living space, more clients or social contacts from people who like your energetic, dynamic approach to life, and possibly less stress because you are more flexible and can adjust to any situation in a world filled with change.

So what would you like to change? The following techniques are designed to limber up your mind to get you thinking about making changes, new connections, and new combinations. Then, when specific situations occur where change is useful you'll be more aware of the possibilities and more creative in coming up with suggestions for effective changes.

Making Changes

The following exercises will give you practice in changing things and trying out new combinations and connections. Use the practice exercises to limber up and then apply these techniques to specific things you want to change. Have a piece of paper and a pencil handy. Perhaps do this brainstorming with others as well.

Technique 1: Changing Objects and Things

This exercise is especially useful when applied to changing material things, like designing an attractive new garden, putting up new paintings or photos on your walls, coming up with new inventions, or developing new product ideas.

To start, practice first by making a list of familiar objects. Look around your room, outside your window, or write down whatever comes to mind. Then think of all the ways you can change that object. Think about its size, color, style, construction, materials, shape, and so forth. Just brainstorm and list any changes you think of. As you mentally make physical changes in the qualities of that object, imagine what it might be used for in its new form. Feel free to think of either practical or fanciful applications. Later, review the ideas to see if any of them might have practical applications. For now you are just exercising your creative idea-generating abilities.

Now apply this technique to an object you actually want to change, such as to create a new or better arrangement for your living room or for a new product. For example, how might you change a smartphone, tablet, or notebook? Maybe you can decorate it to look more unique and express your personality such as adding stickers to the cover. Other possibilities might be attaching some straps so you can carry it over your shoulder or hang it from your neck like a camera. As you brainstorm, don't expect every idea to be useful and practical. Rather, come up with as many ideas as you can as quickly as possible. Later you can eliminate the chaff and select what works.

Technique 2: Places

This exercise is especially useful if you want to change your physical environment, such as for changing landscaping and the look of your home or work environment. For practice, look at a picture or at the scene around you. How many changes can you make? Imagine that you are superimposing another picture over the first and imagine yourself making the changes on this picture. In effect, you are simultaneously looking at or looking back and forth between two scenes—the one that exists and the picture you are changing in your mind's eye. As you look at these two scenes, make any of the following changes:

- Add additional things or people into the scene.
- Take away something or someone.

- Modify or rearrange the things or people in the scene.
- Change the size relationships of the things or people.
- Try a combination of these changes.

Don't worry about making useful changes. You are just practicing. If anything useful comes out of this practice, you can always make these changes later.

Now apply this technique to making changes in some place you really do want to change. For example, suppose you are looking at your living room or at a picture of it. You might mentally add some flowers to a desk, or perhaps see some pictures on the wall, or even imagine hosting a large party. If you look at a garden you might imagine what the area could look like if the garden was no longer there. Likewise, you could see a large building become a small one or even change day into night. The possibilities are as endless as your imagination and creativity.

Visualize these changes in your mind's eye and notice any differences in the mood of the scene or how you feel. You may notice that some settings are more stimulating and exciting than others, and lead people to respond accordingly. For instance, in a bright, cheerful living room with attractive artwork people will be more likely to make comments and compliment you. And the paintings or photographs might help to stimulate conversations as people talk about them or find their own memories stimulated by the images they see. Also, don't feel you must think of only practical ideas. Just let your mental processes flow and generate as many ideas as you can. Later you can select out what's practical and make changes accordingly.

Technique 3: Individuals

This technique is especially useful if you want to change your own appearance to better project the image you want or if you want to change how you interact with or relate to others. For practice, think of all the ways you might change yourself or another person and imagine what might happen if you or they changed in this way. Some things you might want to change are personality traits, interests, hobbies, facial and/or physical appearance, and dress. You can try this exercise wherever you are, wherever you see people, or you can do this by yourself either in your mind's eye or by looking in a mirror. You can practice this technique wherever you are.

Now apply this technique to making changes in yourself or others. For example, look around you and imagine someone you see with different features. Or look in a mirror and imagine yourself with a different look. Another possibility is to combine the features of several different people, including you, into one. Simply imagine what that person would look life if ... and make the change. For example, suppose a man has a mustache or a beard. How would he look without it? How about a woman with long hair? Suppose it were short? An old man? Suppose he were young? A fat woman? What if she were thin? And so on.

Similarly, if you're thinking about changing yourself, as you look in the mirror or at a picture of yourself, imagine how you would look with specific changes, such as wearing different clothes, being heavier or thinner, having a different hairstyle, looking older or younger, with glasses or without, and so on. Later, if you come up with an image you like, you can continue to focus on it from time to time to help make that image become reality (such as an image of yourself twenty pounds lighter).

Finally, to use this technique to influence how you interact with others, look at someone or at a picture of that person and imagine yourself saying different things to them and see that person responding in different ways. You can try this with greetings, with questions, and with making requests for them to do something. Then, if you find a particular approach gets a better response, use that in real life to improve your interaction with that person.

Technique 4: Groups

This is especially useful if you want to change relationships in a so-cial group or a work group. You will do the first part as practice again. Think of any organization or institution you would like to change if you could—ranging from a small social group or activities club to a company, school, or government agency. Then think of all the changes you might make in it. Some of the things you might consider changing could be the number of people, tasks, physical setting, equipment, purpose of the group, activities it engages in, or your role in the group, such as being a leader or coordinator rather than just an ordinary member. Don't worry about making useful changes since you are just practicing, but if anything useful comes out of this you can always make these changes later (or sug-gest them if you're not empowered to make them).

If you are able to make the changes, you might start by writing up the changes you have visualized into the form of a memo or proposal. Then you might share it with others in the organization, such as co-workers or employees, depending on your role in the organization. If others generally like your suggested changes, then you can pursue this more seriously, such as by writing up a more detailed proposal for mak-ing changes or submitting your proposal to a higher-up in the organiza-tion who can become an advocate for the changes you propose. The way to pursue making changes based on what you imagined will de-pend on the nature of your organization and your position and power in it. But to the extent you can, work on making the changes that might actually work to improve the way your organization operates now.

Technique 5: Making New Combinations

This technique is especially useful for creating new decorative schemes for your office or home, inventing new products, or reorganizing a group of people. You can also increase your ability to innovate generally by combining familiar objects or people to create unique arrangements and organizations. To begin, think of two or three familiar objects or people.

You can have an overall goal in mind (such as planning a fun party, creating a new product, or devising a trip for friends), or just work on brainstorming new ideas to get your creative juices flowing and apply this approach to practical situations later.

Now, write down the names of the objects or people. Then, in your mind's eye create a scene with these objects or people. If you have a specific purpose in mind, use that to set the scene. Otherwise, make your scene as wild and fantastic as you wish to activate your creative processes. You can make the objects or people larger or smaller than normal. For instance, say you have chosen Coke bottles, a sink, and some sponges, and want to let your creativity go free. As you look at the bottles you might imagine them as part of a futuristic city where the streets are paved with dishes and the houses are shaped like bottles. Or you might turn the sink and sponges into a harbor with large sponge boats. Let your imagination run completely free, and if you wish, draw a picture of your vision. This approach may seem crazy at first but the process will help you be more creative in applying your ideas to practical matters because your ideas will come more quickly and freely.

Alternatively, if you are trying to come up with a practical result, such as a new product, you might think of how the objects could be combined to do that. For instance, maybe the sponge could be placed around the middle of a bottle to create a floating bottle so people could take their drinks into the pool without the risk of losing them. Whatever your purpose, to use this exercise most effectively let your inner creativity go where it will at first and wait until later to critique your ideas.

Part
Four

Putting
It All
Together

Chapter Eleven

໑

Setting Clear Goals
to Get What You Want

Setting clear and specific goals is another key to getting what you want, since you have to clearly know what you want to get it. It's like traveling to any destination. Know where you are going and follow a map to get there the most convenient and fastest way. Or if you travel around without knowing where you are going or having a map to guide you, you'll get somewhere eventually. But is it where you want to go? Here are a few examples of people who were able to turn their lives around and achieve success once they set clear goals.

Creating a Personal Success Story

Alan was a student at a small university in the South and he felt isolated and alone because of his weight. He had trouble getting women to like him and he wasn't able to participate successfully in some of the activities that appealed to him, like running or canoeing, because he was too heavy. But he had grown used to his heavier weight because his parents and siblings were also overweight due to his mother's cooking. He was used to high calorie meals such as fried chicken, grits, yams, and other southern specialties. But once he set a goal to lose weight, inspired by TV shows like *The Biggest Loser*, his whole life changed. He slimmed down and became more outgoing and confident as a result. Whenever he felt hungry and drawn to reward himself with a big dinner, he clearly visualized his goal again and again and turned away from the temptation.

As part of this visualization, he saw himself going to parties, approaching women, and being comfortable talking to them. He saw himself going to department stores and shops, trying on new trim suits and casual sporty clothes that he could now wear. He also saw himself singing karaoke in front of a group and enjoyed hearing everyone clapping. He visualized himself working off pounds and getting fit at a gym. And he visualized himself at the beach wearing a tight-fitting bathing suit that showed off his new firmer physique. At first these were just visualizations that helped to motivate him to keep going and stay on his diet. But then as he slimmed down, he put these visualizations into practice and he eventually got a new wardrobe, went to the beach in a new bathing suit, and participated in some local karaoke shows feeling confident that he now looked the part.

Therefore, he did much more than just dream about this success in slimming down. Holding this goal clearly before him, he worked on achieving it—and worked hard. It didn't matter to him that this goal was months away because he had nearly fifty pounds to lose. He imagined what he needed to do to get to this goal and began doing it so the pounds melted away—about ten pounds a month.

Finally, after several months his efforts gradually started to pay off as he started to find that women now responded positively to his efforts to talk to them and go on dates with him. And at the same time he developed friendships with other male students who now treated him as an equal to go to events with them, rather than teasing him because he had been so overweight.

Goal-Setting to Achieve
a Successful Work-Life Balance

Sarah, who worked long hours in marketing at a start-up, found that setting goals helped her balance her work and personal life successfully. Most of the other employees in the company were single men who thrived on the long hours. They didn't date much, enjoyed each other's camaraderie, and had no family obligations. But she felt torn because part of her job included extensive social media postings and e-mail exchanges at night, in addition to the sales calls and contacts she made during the day. As a result she had little time for her family. By the time she got home late at night, her young children were already in bed and her husband was tired from the extra responsibilities she had previously handled, such as preparing dinner and getting the kids ready for bed. And in addition to being tired, he increasingly resented her time away from the family so their conversations often turned into arguments about why she had to work so much. Her husband didn't understand why she couldn't simply stop whatever she was doing and come home earlier.

Finally feeling her home life about to implode, Sarah sat down and did some serious thinking. What did she really want out of life for herself? What was most important to her? How could she balance a high-power career with time for her family before she lost it?

After visualizing what she was doing with her life now, and where she wanted to be, Sarah decided she needed to find a work environment with less pressure. As much as she loved her work at the start-up, she realized that nothing was guaranteed. Even with all of her extra effort the start-up might make it or it might not. That meant she could be out of a job at any time, while it was critical for her to spend more time with her family and enjoy her kids' growing up years. So with that realization she decided to look for another job in a more established company. Within two weeks she found one, was given recommendations for doing great work at the start-up, and the company owner's understood why she was leaving since he had his own family that was similarly important to him.

Using Goal-Setting to Get a Promotion

Mary was a receptionist at an ad agency and used goal-setting techniques to be promoted to a copywriter, even though her employer was not encouraging. She had no experience and the agency was only hiring experienced copywriters. Instead of taking no for an answer, she focused on what she wanted. She saw herself working in the copy department and concentrated on what she needed to do to get there. Soon after she started doing this, she learned that the agency was preparing a bid for a new account, and the answer suddenly came to her: submit a sample advertising campaign to the copy chief organizing this effort. On her own time, she started visualizing some ideas for this presentation, worked up a storyboard, and wrote copy based on the vision that came to her. When the copy chief saw these ideas, he was impressed and showed them to the staff working on the project. They incorporated some of these ideas into their sample campaign and when the group got the project they added her as an assistant copywriter.

I have met many others like Alan, Sarah, and Mary who have used various types of GWYW techniques to determine their goals, commit themselves to achieving them, and put their commitment into action. It doesn't matter what the goal is. The key is to have a goal that is realistic and achievable, imagining that you have achieved the goal, determining the steps to achieve it, and finally acting with a firm commitment and assurance to attain that goal. The following techniques will help you select your own goal, decide what you need to do, and begin the process of attaining them.

Deciding What You Want

If you already know what you want and have a realistic goal, you can skip this section. But many people don't know or they want so many things that they can't get it all, or anything, because they lack focus. Then too, some people set up unrealistic, impossible goals for themselves that are really more like pipe dreams—something to wish for, but not something to take seriously—such as living the lavish life of a rich and powerful movie star in Beverly Hills, when in fact, they are a quiet and private type person. Another problem many people have is being too vague about what they want, such as saying, "I want a million dollars." Another obstacle is when people don't feel an intense conviction that they really want something. And some people don't prioritize what they want or determine how important gaining it is to them so they diffuse their energy by going after the less important things rather than concentrating on what they most desire.

To get what you want begin by knowing what that is. In order to gain that clarity and then set your priorities, determine if they are realistic, and create an action plan to go after them, you must do the following:

- Have a clear, specific picture of what you want (for example, I want a job writing copy for one of the big three agencies in town; I want to live in a house renting for about $2,000 in a specific area of the city; I want to spend more time with my family doing fun things on weekends).

- Determine how important your various goals are to you and focus on the more important goals first (go for two or three goals at the same time at the most).

- Determine if your goals are realistically achievable for you.

- Infuse your goal with your feeling of conviction that you really want it, have the ability to achieve it, and are willing to do what it takes to get it.

Since the process begins with gaining clarity, you have to know what you really want now. You can ask yourself the following questions to help you clarify this:

1. What are some things I want right now?

2. What are some things I want in three months? Six months? One year? Five years?

3. What would I like to achieve within the week?

4. What would I like to achieve within one month? Three months? Six months? One year?

5. What is my most important goal or goals?

6. Why is this goal important to me?

7. What other questions are important to me now?

These next few techniques are designed to help you know yourself better so you can make the appropriate decisions about setting your goals.

Visualize the Inner You and Learn What You Want

The purpose of this technique is to discover more clearly who you really are by peeling yourself down to your core like an onion. When you have this information, you are in a better position to know that you truly want a particular goal rather than adopting it because this is something that people around you want. In other words, you are seeking the true you because this is the you that will make the commitment to do what it takes to achieve this goal. But first, this you has to be convinced enough of the value of the goal to make the commitment.

To use this onion peeling technique, get very relaxed, and preferably, lie down. The following can be used as a guide. Just read it to yourself first and then use it as a basic scenario. Or you can read it into a recording device and replay it to direct your experience.

See yourself as a large onion, composed of many layers. On the outside there is a slightly brownish shell. It peels off easily. But as you go down the layers get thicker and thicker, and whiter and whiter. Now, begin to peel, starting with the thin outer layer. This is your outer self. It is the layer of your outer masks and social behavior. As you peel off this layer, see an image representing the other you emerge. Simply observe this image and note it. It doesn't matter now what it means.

Now peel off the next layer. This is the layer of your physical body. It is your material, physical layer. As you peel it off, see another image representing you as your body appears. Again, just observe and note it. Next peel off your middle layer. This is the layer of your intellect, which contains your thoughts. Observe whatever comes to you now. Now down to your fourth layer—the one next to your center. This layer is much thicker and whiter than the others. It is the layer representing your emotions and contains your feelings. Observe the image that comes.

Finally, see yourself peeling apart the last layers and coming down to your core. Now you have arrived at your inner being or spiritual self. Here your inner aspirations reside. Notice the image of you that emerges now. Then, in your mind's eye see a picture of all five images, one on top of the other. What do you notice? Are they similar? Different? Which do you especially like? Are there any you don't? Do the images seem connected? If not, is there anything you can do to make them more consistent or interconnected?

Now focus on the inner level that represents your inner self, or being, and ask yourself, *What do I really want? What will really satisfy me? What can I commit myself to wholeheartedly?* Then observe what images or ideas come. If you get pictures, words, or feelings you don't fully understand, ask yourself what these images or ideas mean, and again relax and be open to whatever comes. You may get full clarification when you are in this relaxed state, but if not, remember these impressions and think about what they mean to you after the experience is over. When you are done count backward from ten, and when you reach one open your eyes feeling refreshed and back in the room. If you wish, record any insights you have gained about yourself.

Use Automatic Writing to Discover What You Want

An alternate approach to learning what you want is by using automatic writing. This is a way of letting go of your conscious mind to let your thoughts flow more spontaneously. Then you can ask yourself questions about anything, including what you want. In addition, you can use this technique to ask further questions, as discussed in the next section, about how to attain your goals once you decide what they are.

To start the process, take a sheet of paper and write down the question you want answered, such as: What do I want? What do I want to achieve? What is my most important goal or goals? Why is this goal important to me?

Next, close your eyes and meditate on this question for a few minutes. Notice any images, words, or phrases that come, but don't try to analyze or understand them yet. After you finish, write down these images and impressions. Next, still in this relaxed state, ask yourself the same question over and over. Phrase it to emphasize that you are probing for the deepest answers. For example: What do I want? What do I really want? What do I really, really want? Write down the first answer to each question that pops into your head. Keep asking the same question until the answers stop coming spontaneously. Then review all your responses. Pay special attention to the last ones as these should come from the deepest part of you, and ask yourself the following questions:

- What do these answers tell you about you and the goals you want?

- How important are these goals?

- How committed are you to achieving them?

- How certain are you that these are realistic goals?

- How convinced are you that you will do what is necessary to attain them?

Believe Your Realistic Goals Will Occur

Besides setting a clear goal, you need to create a goal you can realistically achieve and you must be truly convinced you can obtain it. One way to gain this assurance is to look into your probable future to determine what you are likely to expect. The future is probable because when you look ahead you will see likely alternatives. Any of these might happen because the future isn't fixed. You always have the power to change what you see if you wish to have something else happen. Or you can work toward creating what you see. In essence, the future you perceive represents a projection based on what is happening to you now. If you keep doing what you are doing, certain futures are more likely. On the other hand, you can change the probabilities by changing what you are doing now. You can alter your present to change your future. However, when you have a general sense of what is likely to happen, you are in a better position to plan and develop a series of steps to achieve your goals. The following exercises are designed to help you look ahead and see what is likely to occur. Then you can decide if that is what you want or not and act accordingly.

Where Am I Likely to Be?

Get relaxed using any relaxation technique and close your eyes. Then imagine that you are drawing energy in from all around you, and feel this energy coming in and infusing you with wisdom and clarity. You might imagine you are drawing energy from the earth up through your feet and energy from the air down through your head. Experience this energy coming together within your body as a brilliant beam of light, which vitalizes your whole being and helps you feel wise and all-knowing.

Now, as the energy continues to flow through you look around. You are in a train station, but it is a unique station. The train consists of six sleek, silver cars that run on a monorail and their destination is a time, not a place. You can see the sign on the station platform. It says "Destination: The Future."

This train will take you there so climb on one of the cars and decide where in the future you want to go. Two months ahead, six months, one year, two years, or more? The train can travel up to ten years ahead. Now lean back and go. The ride is very smooth and fast. Places, people, train stations whizz by quickly like a blur. You barely see them as you pass, and then you are there. Now step out and into future time. Notice what or who is around you. What are you doing? Is this what you want to do? Ask yourself any questions you want about what your life is like now. Then wait for each answer. When you have learned all you want, step back onto the train. If you wish, travel onward to another time period or return to the present and come back to normal consciousness.

After this experience, ask yourself questions about the future you have seen. How do you feel about this future? Do you want this? If so, think about what you can do to best achieve this goal. If not, consider creating an alternate future and changing your present so you can create the kind of future you really want.

What Is Likely to Happen?

This technique is useful both in thinking about long-term goals and assessing the outcome of everyday activities. You ask yourself what is likely to happen tomorrow, next month, next year—any time frame you want to know about. Then, if you like what is probable you can either relax or do what is necessary to make that happen. If not, you can intervene to find a new, more desirable direction.

Get relaxed and close your eyes to begin the process. Once you feel ready, visualize yourself in a small, dark room. You are seated in a large, comfortable chair in front of a small table. One small light glows in the room and casts its light on the table. There you see a large crystal ball that is round and firm, or if you prefer, see a large computer screen that is lit up.

Now, put your hands around the crystal or on the computer console. As you do so, feel the energy of whatever you are touching throb with power. It's like a radio receiver receiving energy waves from the universe. Whenever you ask it a question, it will light up with an image or you will hear a voice with your answer. Now ask your question. What will happen at a certain time? What will the outcome of something be? Then wait for your answer. It will appear as an image in the crystal ball or on the screen, or a voice will speak to you. When that fades, ask additional questions if you wish. When you finish, the image of the crystal ball or computer console will fade. Afterward, write down your prediction and think about it. Is this something you want? If not, what can you do to change it?

How Realistic Are My Goals?

This is a quick technique to assess the practicality of your goals after you have decided what you want or have considered what is likely to happen. This technique is especially useful when you either hope something will happen or are afraid something will and aren't sure. For example, suppose you are hoping for a new promotion or a new job. You might ask if you are likely to get it. Or suppose you are thinking about moving and aren't sure if you can afford to move to a nicer place with higher rent. You think you want it, but you don't know if this is a realistic goal for now. Or what if you aren't sure if it is time to settle down by getting married and if this person is the one? This technique can help you decide.

There are two versions of this technique. Use the approach that feels more comfortable for you. In one, you use the crystal ball or computer screen method just described to ask yes and no questions. In the other, you ask your body for yes and no cues.

The Crystal Ball/Computer Screen Technique

This approach begins like the "What is Likely to Happen?" technique just described. You imagine a crystal ball or computer screen before you and ask a question, such as, *Will I get the job? Should I take the more expensive apartment? Do I want to get married now? Is this the person I want to spend the rest of my life with?* However, instead of seeing an image or hearing a voice with a message for your answer, you simply see or hear the words yes, no, maybe, or not sure.

The Body Cues Technique

This technique takes a little practice to develop accuracy, but once you are accustomed to it you can get your answer in a few seconds. Essentially, you are reading your own body for answers, as your body holds the key to your subconscious. But first you have to train your body to give those cues.

Initially, you need to physically move your body to get your answers. However, after some practice you can visualize these bodily movements in your mind. Or you can develop a voice inside you to answer for your body. To get your body accustomed to giving you answers, use the following procedure to get your responses physically. Later, go through this process in your mind.

Stand straight and imagine your body as a pendulum. Now sway backward and forward. That means yes. Sway to the right and to the left. That means no. Sway in a circular motion. That means you are not sure or can't answer now.

Practice these motions until you are familiar with the signals. Then ask yourself some simple yes/no questions that you know the answer to. Your body should respond with the appropriate swaying motion. Once it does so consistently, you are ready to begin asking it for answers. Now ask your questions about your goals as yes/no questions and learn either if your goals are realistic or if they are in your best interest. For example, ask, *Is my goal (state it clearly) likely to happen?* Or, *Is this a realistic goal to have at this time?* Or ask, *Should I have this goal?* Or, *Is this a beneficial goal for me to pursue at this time?*

After you ask each question, observe how your body responds—with a yes motion, a no, or a maybe. With practice you should get clear yeses or nos. Once you do you can decide whether to act accordingly.

If you get a lot of circular motions (maybes) or get alternating yeses and nos to the same question, you may not be asking the question clearly or your personality may be getting in the way. To find out, simply ask, *Is my question unclear?* Or, *Is my personality getting in the way?* If so, either clarify or reframe your question.

Prioritizing Your Goals

If you have developed a number of goals that you can realistically achieve, decide how important these goals are to you, as you can only focus effectively on a few goals at a time. Also, it is often helpful to have an overall goal that is most important to you as this helps to give you a sense of direction and focus. Then, with this primary orientation you can concentrate your energy on achieving your purpose. This process is much like concentrating your energy like a laser beam as compared to the scattered light emitted by a flashlight. Scattered light will reach the same target but it is diffused, whereas the laser beam will pierce right through with its intense burning light.

For example, if you have a family your primary goal might be to spend time doing something together on the weekend and find different activities you will enjoy doing together. If you have recently moved to a new area, your goal might be to get involved in local activities and social groups. If you are working for a company, your goal might be to complete a series of tasks effectively so you are in line for a promotion. If you have your own business or are a freelance professional, your goal might be to attract or attain a certain number of customers or clients each month and do whatever is necessary to get more business.

If you aren't already clear on the relative importance of your goals, this technique will help you rate your goals and prioritize them.

What Are My Most Important Goals?

Take a sheet of paper and a pencil and write these headings across the top: My Goals, Their Importance to Me, My Most Important Goals, and Rating My Most Important Goals. Next draw a line between each of these headings so you have four columns

Then get calm and relaxed using any method that works for you. You want to be in a quiet, meditative frame of mind to do this process. Then, as quickly as you can, write down all your goals. Don't try to think about them or judge them. Some goals may be very general, some very specific, some long-term, and some short-term. It doesn't matter. Just write down whatever comes to you. You will probably write down some of the goals you have already come up with in previous exercises, but you may find that other goals surface as well. Keep going until you feel yourself slowing down. Then concentrate for perhaps another minute until you feel finished.

Now look down this list quickly and rate each goal in order based on how important it is to you using a rating scale of ten (most important) to zero (least important). Put down the first impression that comes to mind as you do this in the second column on the same line as that goal. Don't think about your reasons for giving a particular rating—just let your inner self respond intuitively. Your immediate response will give you an accurate picture of how important that goal is to you. Next list your goals with the highest rating in the third column. Start with any tens and list them, next any nines, and so on until you have written down three or more goals. Stop after you have listed at least three goals—just be sure to include all the goals in the last numerical category listed.

Finally, look at this list of your most important goals, and as quickly as you can, rank them in order from one (most important) to three (least important). Don't worry about the other goals on your list. You are interested in the three most important goals to you. Also, don't try to think as you rank your goals. Just react as quickly as possible to tap your inner feelings.

The result of this exercise should be discovering the goal that is most important to you so you can focus on what you need to do to achieve this goal. Then, if you have additional time to devote to working on your goals, you can try to attain goals two or three as well. But put your emphasis on goal number one. This is your most important goal so that's what you should go after accomplishing first.

Developing the Conviction You Will Achieve Your Goal

Once you are clear on what you want, know it is realistic, and are certain this is your most important goal, you need to regularly energize it with your conviction that you will achieve this goal and you will do what is necessary to achieve it. I have done this repeatedly in finding a new place to live where I could write as well as entertain guests. I focused very clearly on what I wanted and got a picture of where I wanted to be—first in San Francisco, then in Oakland, then in Santa Monica, then back in San Francisco, and most recently, to a small house in Lafayette. I even picked out a small neighborhood where I wanted to move and repeatedly visualized myself finding a place and living there. Furthermore, I imagined moving in as of a certain date, but not before because I was paying rent somewhere else until then. Once I was ready to move, within a few days of looking I found exactly the place I wanted, much like Julie described in an earlier chapter, by driving by and looking for rent signs or most recently finding the listing online. And each time I visualized what to say or offer to the landlord to get him to rent to me, so each time, of all the people looking, I was the one to get the house or apartment. Each time I had a clear picture of exactly where I wanted to be down to the neighborhood and even within a few block area, what kind of house or building I wanted to be in, how much space I wanted, and how I wanted to set up the different rooms. Within a few days I had located the place, furnished it in my mind, and a few weeks later I moved in and turned my visualization of where I wanted to be into a reality.

In a similar example, Edward was fully convinced that Charlene was the woman he wanted to marry, though she was wavering about making that commitment since she wasn't quite ready to settle down. She still wanted to see the world and would maybe think about marriage afterward. Edward worried about her meeting others and maybe choosing someone else when she was ready to make a commitment. But Edward was so strong in his conviction that she was the right one for him that he took some time to visualize what he might do to win her hand. The result was that he saw himself giving her a ticket for a six-week trip around the world that summer and even saw the beautiful forest grove where he would give her this.

On their next date a week later he drove to a nearby park, and in the beauty of the redwoods, he led her to a grove by a creek where he presented her with the ticket to enjoy a wonderful trip through Europe, Asia, and Australia—all the places she said she wanted to go—and when she returned he hoped to marry her. She was so touched that she immediately said yes and after she returned they had a beautiful wedding and reception that featured photos that she had taken during her trip. Likewise, you need to be fully convinced that you will get what you want and will find the method to do so, and then you will! The following exercise is designed to help you develop this feeling of conviction.

Becoming Convinced

Get relaxed and close your eyes. Find a few minutes during the day when you can do this, or do it when you are drifting off to sleep or right after you wake up.

Then concentrate with all your attention on realizing your goal. See your goal already achieved. For example, if it is a material possession see yourself owning and enjoying it; if it is a new job or business, see yourself in your new role; if it is a new place, see yourself in this new environment. Make your images of your goal as clear as possible. Be aware of everything you see: colors, objects, people, rooms, furnishings, and so on. Listen to what you hear around you: sounds, voices, and conversations. Touch objects around you. Notice anything you smell, taste, sense moving, and so forth. Experience achieving your goal as fully as possible. In fact, you might imagine yourself as the director of a movie on location, shaping everything as you want it right now—and you are the actor in a starring role!

Then, as you see this goal achieved very vividly, say to yourself, *I will achieve this goal. I will do what is necessary to get it. This goal is completely possible. I just need to act to get it, and it will happen now!*

Finally, end this visualization and return to normal consciousness feeling totally convinced and certain you will get what you want. This feeling will stay with you during the day and help you take the necessary steps to achieve your goal.

Determining the Steps to Your Goal

To attain an overall goal, break it down into specific objectives or steps to be accomplished and be aware of what kind of resources you might need along the way. For example, if you have decided to take up skiing, some of the things that may be required are:

- A new wardrobe with ski wear, including ski pants, a jacket, and boots.
- Skiing equipment you can buy or rent.
- A skiing class to develop the new skills.
- A few extra days of vacation leave from your company so you can drive to the location where you will be skiing.
- Arrangements for a cabin where you and your friends will stay for the weekend.

If you are thinking of starting a small business, you may need to take some of the following steps:

- Doing a location study to determine the best place to set up your business.

- Reviewing the tasks required to decide who you need to hire.

- Writing up a budget indicating your expected costs and likely income to show what you need to charge for your products or services.

- Assessing how long before you can expect to make a profit and how much you need for now to get your business going.

You also need to work out the sequence of what you will do when and prioritize each of the activities in your plan. Then if you find you can't do everything you wish, you can drop out the activities with a lower priority. The following techniques will help you decide what you need to do, the resources you require to do this, how to order these activities, and how to prioritize these plans so you can carry out your action plan most efficiently.

Deciding the Steps to My Goal

First, get a sheet of paper and pencil and write the goal you want to accomplish on top. Next make four columns entitled: What I Need to Do, Resources I Need, Order of Execution, and Importance of Activity. Then, with this before you, take some time to get relaxed and focused. Once you feel completely calm and in a meditative frame of mind, begin.

Start by thinking of all the things you need to do to reach your goal. Don't try to judge how important these activities are. Just write down everything that comes to you in the first column: What I Need to Do. Leave a few lines between each activity so you can fill in the resources list in the next column. Keep brainstorming and coming up with ideas until you feel finished.

Next go to the second column: Resources I Need. Now look at each thing you need to do, and next to it list any resources necessary. Again, don't try to judge or evaluate your thoughts. Just write them down. Keep going until you feel finished with each one, and if you don't need anything special for a particular activity, go on to the next.

Now go to the third column: Order of Execution, where you will number the activities listed in the first column in sequence. Begin with what you should do first, then number the second, the third, and so forth. If you're not sure of the order or feel you will do some activities around the same time, give them the same number.

Finally, go to the last column: Importance of Activity. Again, look at the activities in column one and as quickly as possible, rate them as to their importance according to A (very important), B (important), and C (do if possible). When you are done, return to your everyday state of consciousness.

Now take the information you have acquired to create an activities list for yourself. List the goal you are going to achieve at the top of the page (such as, a promotion at work or doubling the size of my business). Then, in order using the numbers you have listed in column three, write down the activities you plan to do and the resources you need to do them. Next to each one write the letter indicating the importance of this activity to help you do this. For instance, if you are seeking to take a much-needed vacation to Australia and learn to snorkel, your goals list might look something like this:

1. Sign up for a class on snorkeling   A
   Resources needed: $200 class fee

2. Get some new clothes for the warmer weather   A
   Resources needed: $1,000 for new clothes

3. Arrange travel arrangements with a local travel agent   A
   Resources needed: $4,000 for the trip

4. Get a new camera to take still photos and videos   A
    Resources needed: $1,000 for the camera

5. Join a travel club to share memories and photos   B
    Resources needed: $100 for membership fee

Start Now!

Once you know your goal, are committed to achieving it, and know what you need to do to get it, the final step is to START NOW!

Perhaps use some of the energy-raising techniques described in chapter 3 to infuse yourself with the energy you need to get started with enthusiasm. Maybe use some of the techniques described in chapter 7 to build your confidence that you will attain your goal.

Then, with conviction, commitment, and a one-pointed focus, begin the process of getting what you want. Know you'll get it. Believe you can do it. Do what is necessary to accomplish your goal, and you will! That's the magic of these GWYW techniques. By thinking, imagining, and knowing what you want you will mobilize yourself to take the appropriate actions to get it. In effect, you are creating the situation necessary to attain what you desire. The outcome you want starts within you!

Believe You Can Do It

Besides clearly knowing what you want, knowing it is achievable, determining the steps to get it, and going after it, you also need to have a belief in yourself. It's that *can do* confidence. Many people don't get what they want because they don't believe in themselves enough. They don't believe they can get what they want. In turn, they don't want anything enough to try and get it. They may set a goal, but only half-heartedly work toward it so the outcome is usually a half-hearted result, the wrong result, or no result at all.

A good example of this is the person who says he or she wants to lose weight but continually stops trying, regains the weight, and resumes the diet only to succumb to temptation and start to eat the wrong things again. Others set no goals at all and remain stuck in situations they don't like. An example of this is the person who hates his town or job but doesn't move, too afraid to try something new. By contrast, the person with a clear goal and commitment to it can overcome all sorts of obstacles to achieve it. Such as the many stories of miraculous survival in winter storms, days at sea, and other devastating conditions. The belief that they can do it for themselves, or for others, keeps them going when someone without this belief might easily have perished. There's even a website that features these incredible stories of survival: www.wildernesssurvivalstories.com, and the stories are sent to the site from all over the world. When you recognize your inner power you suddenly gain confidence and are motivated to go after and get what you want.

Overcoming Fear to Change Your Life

Anyone can make this transformation to belief. Even those who have been stuck in negative thinking for most of their lives. Even when things seem very grim and hopeless, once you start using GWYW thinking you can break through all sorts of blocks.

Overcoming Fear for Personal Transformation

Harriet discovered the ability to overcome a long-term fearful mind-set when she encountered a crisis in her own life. She was an independent, long-widowed woman in her late fifties who had retired and enjoyed the freedom of not having to work, though she volunteered at a local hospital. She frequently got together with relatives and friends, enjoyed shopping and gardening, and though she lived alone she was never lonely, but then she fell and fractured her hip. After she returned from the hospital wearing a large lower body cast, she had to hire people to care for her. Though the doctor explained she would be in a cast for about six weeks and could return to her normal routine, Harriet turned the incident into a three-year disaster. Instead of focusing on what she really wanted—to get better and strengthen her ability to do so—she let her fear she wouldn't succeed overwhelm her, leading her to create the very problems she feared. Her hip took longer to heal than expected and she began to fear being alone. She alienated her friends and relatives by rejecting their help and criticizing what they did. Soon she was extremely depressed and unaware of her role in creating these problems, so she began dwelling on her lack of ability to do anything. And since she had less and less contact with others, she directed her anger inward. When relatives and doctors tried to help her, she resisted their help insisting that her situation was hopeless, no one could understand what she was experiencing, and no one could help. Harriet lost all confidence in herself and didn't realize the underlying problem was her own negative attitude.

At her lowest point, facing a do-or-die crisis, she let go of her defeatist attitude and realized that only her own will could change her circumstances. She was then able to tap into her own inner power, and once she did she was able to pull herself together, join a group program at the hospital, and began to look at what she could do to help herself. Within a few weeks the transformation was dramatic. She began calling her friends and relatives telling them she felt great. Suddenly she felt she could do anything. She had been to the very bottom and had pulled herself out. Now she wanted to pass on this message. She had done it so she now believed in herself, realizing she could take back her personal power. She had only to reach out and do this and it would be there. By believing this power was there, she could make it hers.

Underlying this transformation was a changed belief in herself. In thinking all was hopeless, Harriet lost faith in her ability to help herself, and so she couldn't help herself. Her actions reinforced her beliefs so she continued to feel helpless, friendless, and alone. But once her attitude changed and she realized she had to help herself, Harriet came to believe she could do it and found she could. So now her actions strengthened her inner confidence and helped to empower her even further as she reached out to others and regained a sense of purpose and direction in life through helping others. In turn, these actions helped her realize how much she could do, empowering her to do even more.

The Circle of Empowerment Yields Positive Results

The interplay between Harriet's empowering beliefs that triggered her empowering actions, and the success of these actions that reinforced her beliefs, illustrate this circle of reinforcement where beliefs lead to actions, which support those beliefs. As you can see, if you believe in yourself and trust in your power to produce desired results, you will create the experiences to support that belief. If you believe you are attractive and people are attracted to you, you will exude that aura of confidence and act as if you expect their interest, and people will be drawn to you. If you are convinced you should have a certain job or promotion, you will express a feeling of assurance and act as if you belong in that job so fellow workers and employers will think of you in that role.

Believe in Yourself to Empower Yourself

Instead of giving in to fears and feelings of I can't, turn those fears and feelings around and say I can. How? To overcome your fear and the I can't feeling, try acting as if you really can. When you act as if you believe you can, you empower yourself to do the thing you fear. That's because when you act as if you believe in yourself, that action helps turn your belief into reality. Even if you don't really believe it at first, nurture and reinforce that belief by taking on new tasks and responsibilities. Then your success will empower you and thereby strengthen your belief in yourself so you can better reach your desired goals. You must believe and trust in your own power. If at first you don't believe it, create that belief by acting as if you do.

Say I Can and Gain the Support of Others

Besides increasing your own confidence and self-esteem as described in chapter 7, saying I can is a powerful way to gain the support and skills of others who are attracted to working with a person with a can do attitude. Such support, in turn, works to further expand what you can accomplish.

That's what happened when Jim was trying to revive membership in a local social meet-up group for singles over thirty-five. The previous organizer had gotten very busy with his work and other activities and had let the group languish. He planned fewer activities and only set up monthly happy hours instead of the full range of activities he planned when the group started. Yet, Jim really liked the people he met in the group so he offered to become an assistant organizer so he could plan some activities himself. At first the organizer resisted, concerned he was losing control of the group. But Jim contacted him again after a few weeks, pointing out how the group was dying without a new infusion of energy. So finally the organizer relented and Jim began planning new unique trips to reinvigorate the group, such as a day at an amusement park and a visit to a historic mansion that was supposedly occupied by a ghost. The result was that membership sign ups for the new activities increased, and after a few months the original organizer turned over the group to Jim and simply participated as a regular member. So through his determination and I can attitude, Jim succeeded not only in reviving the group but also in becoming its new leader.

Focus on Your Good Qualities and Empower Yourself

This leading by action approach works because the action creates or reinforces the belief. If you believe something, it will lead you to act to support that belief, and if that belief is correct the result will reinforce the belief. For example, if you believe you will be good in a particular sport, such as running, archery, or fencing, because you have the right kind of physique you will usually be able to pursue that sport successfully. That's because that knowledge will give you the confidence to start taking classes and develop the necessary techniques. And as you find you can easily apply what you learn in the lessons, that will reinforce the belief in your ability to do well in the sport, so you will do more to practice and become even better. Visualizing yourself getting better as you practice the skill will contribute to your progress as well. That's because actions that simulate being based on a belief can often produce the same successful results as actions based on a belief. That successful outcome then helps to create and reinforce the belief.

By contrast, if you don't believe you can do something you may act hesitantly, reflecting your lack of certainty. If that's the case, create some reinforcing experiences to help you overcome that uncertainty. Think of the popular claim, "If you believe you are great, you are great … If you believe you can do it, you can."

But what if you aren't really sure? How can you create the supporting experiences you need? How can you act as if you truly believe? How can you put aside your feelings of uncertainty and create the experiences that will support that belief?

One way to push past your fears—to take an action you want, affirm a belief in yourself, or have a greater sense of power generally—is to focus on your good qualities and on what you can do to remind yourself you can do certain things, and then you can. That's what happened for Nancy, a dental assistant who felt bored and unfulfilled. Though she dreamed of starting a jewelry design business, she was afraid to leave her secure position and instead kept thinking about the barriers to her goal. Most notably her limited funds and experience, though underneath these concerns was her fear that she didn't have the ability. For several years she continued to work as a dental assistant. Then, at a workshop one weekend, she learned how to imagine what she wanted and saw herself pushing aside all the barriers. In her imagination there were no I can'ts and no fears standing in her way. Instead, she focused on the qualities and abilities she had that could help her achieve her goal and how she could put these into practice.

She listed a good sense of design, knowledge of what people like, persistence, strong commitment to complete things once she choose to do them, good ability to organize and direct people, and so on in her mind and wrote them down. Then with these qualities in mind, she began imagining the steps she would need to take to start a business. She would need to hire a part-time assistant to sell her jewelry to stores and wholesalers, turn a room in her house into an office and workshop, create a letterhead and flyers, and so on. As she visualized these possibilities, she realized she could start part-time. Then once she built up the business she could quit her job and do it full-time. Focusing on what she had and could do gave her the confidence she needed to begin working toward her real desire. Then empowered by this changed focus, she put a series of actions into practice, which made her feel even more confident that she could achieve her goal.

Like Nancy, you can focus on what you want and on the steps you need to take to achieve your desire. Begin by focusing on the skills and abilities you have that can help you reach that goal. Push away the I can'ts—thoughts about skills and abilities you don't have. Remind yourself you can always learn those skills, you can find someone who has them, or you may find they may not be that necessary. See those barriers falling away.

Next write down all the qualities and abilities you bring to what you want to do and think about the steps you must take to make it happen. Use the brainstorming technique (see chapter 10) to come up with ideas. Write them down, rate them, then set priorities and a timeline indicating what you need to do and when. As you proceed, continue to remind yourself that you can achieve your goal because you have all the qualities and abilities you need (or know where to find them). You can use the following exercise to help you recognize your good qualities and use them to achieve your goal.

Use Your Good Qualities to Reach Your Goal

The following exercise will help build your feelings of empowerment by concentrating on the positive things you bring to any situation. This helps reinforce your belief in yourself and your desire to reach your goal as you see yourself achieving it. The process is a bit like building the foundation of a house and solidifying the structure. You need to shore it up with various supports, including your good qualities, your desire to do something, your belief that you can do it, and your vision of doing what you want to do. Each of these four elements helps to support the structure—the goal you want to achieve. Eliminate or weaken any of these elements and you weaken the structure and your ability to achieve your goal. The focus on your good qualities is the bedrock. It helps to strengthen and shore up the rest.

The following exercise will help you to become more aware of, acknowledge, and embrace your good qualities (personality traits, talents, accomplishments, and so forth). Do this exercise whenever you are faced with a difficult task, new responsibilities, or a conflict or problem.

Start by closing your eyes and getting relaxed. Concentrate on your breathing for a minute or two to calm down. Now, ask yourself each of the following questions and listen receptively to whatever comes. *What are the personality traits I am most proud of? What are the talents I am most proud of? What are the accomplishments I am most proud of?*

Quickly write down whatever comes to mind. Keep going until you have at least ten traits, talents, and accomplishments listed. If you slow down or can't think of anything, ask the question again. Remain focused and concentrate on all your good qualities and all the good things you have done.

Next, review your list. As you read each item create a mental picture of yourself with that quality, talent, or accomplishment. See yourself and experience yourself having that quality, using that talent, and achieving that accomplishment. Let yourself feel good as you do. Then think about the current goal or problem you want to resolve. Remind yourself that you can do it because you have all these qualities, talents, and accomplishments.

Now imagine this desired goal or problem on a big white screen in front of you and ask yourself, *What qualities or talents do I have that I can use to help me achieve this goal or resolve this problem?* Let the answers come to you and write down whatever comes. These may be qualities or talents you have already listed or they may be new ones.

Now imagine yourself achieving your goal or resolving your problem. See the goal attained or the problem resolved. Praise yourself and feel good about achieving or resolving it. (You may want to see yourself receiving an award or reward for what you have done.) Remind yourself that you have been able to do this because of all your good qualities, talents, and accomplishments.

Finally, return to the room feeling very good for all you have, all you have done, and all you can do in the future.

Focus on the Qualities You Want to Develop and Empower Yourself

In addition to focusing on the qualities you already have, you can feel more power by imagining that you already have the qualities you want to develop, and by doing so, experience having those qualities. This means imagining that you already have the personality traits, talents, or abilities you want and that you have already achieved those future goals. You are using the affirmation process to tell yourself you have the qualities you want to develop and you go beyond simple affirmations to focus your energy on experiencing these desired qualities. Then you begin to feel you have these qualities. Likewise, by changing your attitude about yourself, you change your actions to match your attitude. You begin to trust that you could be the way you want to be, and as you act this way, others perceive and respond to you differently. Thus, by using this technique you change your own feelings about yourself, the way you act, and the way others act toward you. In this way, the imaginative process helps to turn your desires into beliefs that get turned into action.

By using affirmations you are inserting another step at the beginning of the circle of empowerment process by pre-visualizing what you want to be and turning what you envision into belief. You can see this process below showing how you go from imaging desired results to empowering beliefs that lead to desired results.

As the visualization process creates that belief, you feel more confidence because you believe in yourself. Then, by affirming that you have what you want with the intensity of focus that creates belief you can help overcome the fears and barriers standing in your way and make what you want happen.

You can use the following exercise to help you do this.

Affirming Your Beliefs about Yourself and Your Future Goals

To prepare, create three columns and head one of them "Qualities I Want to Develop," the second "Goals I Want to Achieve," and the third "Problems I Want to Solve." Then you will create a list in each column as you get answers to your questions, including how these qualities and goals can help you solve any problems you list.

Now ask yourself each of these questions and listen receptively to whatever comes: *What are the qualities (traits, talents, or abilities) I most want to develop now? What are the accomplishments I most want to achieve now? What is the problem I most want to solve now?*

Quickly write down the first few qualities and accomplishments that come to mind. List about four or five of each. Then, looking at this list, choose whatever is most important to you and write that as an affirmation of something you already have, as if you had that trait, talent, or ability or as if you had already accomplished the thing you want or had resolved the problem you want to resolve. Make your affirmation in the present tense even though you don't really have that thing or quality, because we create beliefs based on how we see ourselves and those beliefs turn into actions and realities.

After you finish writing the affirmation, focus on it for one or two minutes. Close your eyes and repeat your affirmation over and over to yourself. As you do, see it and feel it happening. Imagine it is a movie you are in and you are playing the part. It is unrolling on the screen before your eyes. As you experience it, imagine you are sending all your concentrated energy to the image on your mental screen. Energize it, make it happen, turn up the volume, make the picture even more intense, maybe add surround sound or smells—make the experience vital and alive.

Finally, release the experience and return to the present knowing that you are turning that experience into a true belief and making it happen. Repeat your affirmations over a period of time to reinforce them, make them truly real for you, and integrate them into yourself so they become a part of you. Then you can put them into practice.

Do this exercise daily for about a week for each affirmation you work with while you are trying to develop a new quality, accomplish something, or resolve a problem. As you practice you'll notice that the affirmation becomes more and more a part of you, and as it does you will feel a greater sense of confidence and empowerment as you turn what you want to be or have into what is.

How to Overcome Past Failures

Even if you have experienced failures, you can put those aside and move on. The key is to regard any failure as an opportunity for learning and a stepping-stone to future success so you don't remain stuck in the image of having failed. Remember, the failure is not you. You may have failed at doing something but that is just one experience or event in your life, not the only experience or event. It does not define who you are. You are not a failure because you have experienced a failure. Tell yourself that and think about how you can learn from that experience to change something you do in the future to be more successful and move on.

For example, many now-successful movie stars have gone through a period of failure before soaring to great heights. At one time, Jeremy Renner, who gained fame from his roles in *The Hurt Locker* and *The Bourne Legacy*, lived in near-poverty. As a struggling actor he lived on a $5-a-week diet of noodles, doughnuts, and McDonald's, and for a time slept in his car. In her early twenties, Halle Berry lived in homeless shelters. Before becoming famous, Leonardo DiCaprio was constantly in debt and couldn't even find a well-paying job. It took him years to obtain solid acting gigs and he spent most of his time with local prostitutes and drug dealers before he finally found success.

If you too have felt like a failure, don't stay in that rut. You can put that failure behind you by following these steps:

- Take some time to think about what happened to cause the failure and then think about how you can change the situation or yourself.

- Be specific about what you need to change. If, for example, you feel it is something you did, ask yourself what exactly it was.

- Select no more than two or three things to change at any one time. Make these changes before going on to make any others.

- As you make each change, imagine your experience or experiences of failure as going back further and further in the past and being further and further away from you.

- Experience yourself becoming a new you.

Experiencing Your Goal Achieved

Begin by closing your eyes and getting relaxed. Take a minute or two to focus on your breathing until you feel calm and relaxed.

Now, imagine there is a large, empty screen in front of you and see an image of the way you want things to be on it. See yourself having achieved your goal or having resolved your problem. Whatever it is, it's happening right now and you are experiencing it fully. As you see it happening, put yourself in the picture. You are acting and interacting with others. Notice what's occurring. What do you hear? How do you feel?

Meanwhile, as you intensely experience all of this happening, notice how good you feel about achieving your goal. You feel very satisfied and very powerful. You feel excited, energized, strong, and very self-confident. You feel fully in charge.

Now, notice others coming up to you or calling to congratulate you. They praise you for your success and you feel warm and glowing as you receive praise. They tell you how proud they are of you for what you have accomplished. You feel wonderful, full of power, and able to do anything you want in the future. Take a minute or so to bask in this feeling of accomplishment and to re-experience attaining your desired goal. Then, when you feel ready, let this picture go and return to the room and everyday consciousness. You should now feel clear about what to do and ready to work toward your goal.

Putting It All Together

The exercises in this chapter can be used alone or together to help you envision and achieve your goal. Should you feel any barrier to moving toward that goal, other exercises will help you feel greater confidence, self-esteem, and empowerment so you feel better about yourself and are better able to achieve your goals. These exercises work by adding a charge of energy and focused attention. By repeatedly visualizing and affirming what you want, and projecting your will and firm conviction that the result you want has already occurred, you begin to act in ways that further reinforce your beliefs. That conviction, in turn, leads to further actions based on these beliefs and so on around the circle of empowerment where beliefs lead to actions that reinforce beliefs. By imagining changed actions, results, or beliefs, you can actually affect the outcome of events.

Chapter Twelve

✿

Make the "Write" Decisions

Getting what you want means making the right decisions—both about what you want and how to get there. Coming up with a variety of alternatives and selecting the best one (as described in chapter 10) can be one way to reach a decision. But sometimes you have difficulty choosing among the alternatives, or there may be no alternatives; only the option of saying yes, no, or deferring the decision to a later time when you are more ready to decide.

For instance, say you are trying to decide where to move. Should you take that three-bedroom apartment in a great location and seek a roommate to help with the costs? Should you rent that one-bedroom that is in a better location though it's smaller and more expensive? Should you stay put until you can afford something better? Or should you consider moving to another city where the costs will be much less though you will have to commute an hour or more a day? Which option should you choose?

We make decisions all the time—sometimes with very little or no thought—and that's fine if we're deciding whether or not to turn right or left as we walk down the street, pick up this or that while shopping, watch this or that TV program, and so forth. But when it comes to the important decisions such as which job to take, whether to move, whether to change careers, or whether to seek a promotion we sometimes get stuck. We may not realize that there are more possibilities than we're considering so we limit our choices.

Sometimes it's hard to decide, and you feel you don't have the ability or time to work out your decision logically by weighing all the pros and cons and then deciding. In fact, logic can sometimes get in the way of making the right gut-level decision that satisfies your inner self. That's when it helps to tap directly into your unconscious or intuition to make that gut choice that expresses what you really want. As it's sometimes difficult to hear that inner voice, the exercises in this chapter are designed to help you both trigger that inner response and listen to what it says to do.

How Intuition Techniques Work

These techniques work by altering your consciousness so that you pay attention to your unconscious, or intuition, and respond accordingly, as previously discussed, and briefly recapped here. Your intuition can talk to you in a number of ways: through automatic writing, through visual symbols or thoughts, and through signals from your body. Different people get their information for making decisions in different ways, and the way you get information may change under different circumstances.

For example, when I first began working with these techniques I used automatic writing for making more important decisions such as choosing among different work projects when I couldn't do everything and had to make a choice. Now though, the process occurs more quickly just in my thoughts, which commonly occurs when these techniques become internalized. But when I began using this process I only occasionally called on this ability perhaps once or twice a month, so it retained its specialness for me. When I used it, I typically took a minute or two to get relaxed, ask a question, and write down whatever answers

I received. After this first question, my writing took the form of a dialogue between my inner voice and me, and I wrote down whatever it said. For instance, it might say something like:

> You're thinking of doing too many projects right now. There's a risk of getting scattered and doing nothing very well. So choose. We know it's difficult, but select the project you feel is most important to you. What is it that you ask? Well, for right now we think…

Afterward I read over what I wrote and used this advice to make a decision, and usually did what my writing as advised. Also, from time to time I read over past messages and reviewed them in light of the outcome that resulted when I followed the advice. It was a way of further verifying the value of the technique by looking back to see that I had gotten good advice—which I usually had.

Some people prefer to get advice by going on mental journeys or by mentally asking a counselor for assistance. For instance, Pam, an administrative assistant and part-time student, imagines herself entering a workshop on her home computer. She presses a button and an image of her counselor appears on the monitor. He looks a little like a college physics professor with a thin face, small goatee, graying hair, and pipe. Then she asks him questions and the answers appear on the screen.

One time she consulted with her counselor when she wasn't sure whether to leave her current boyfriend, suggest they try dating others, or have a discussion with him about making some changes in their relationship. His advice was to have that discussion about making changes and then be ready to suggest seeing others for a while or walk away from the relationship entirely, depending on her boyfriend's responses. If he didn't want to discuss anything, it was time to leave.

Andrea, an administrative assistant, often takes a long mental trip to see an old man on a mountain for advice. She begins by seeing herself in a beautiful meadow and then walks along a path that leads through the woods into the mountains. After a while she comes to a small mountain cabin and inside meets a wise man who knows the answers to whatever she asks. He invites her in for tea, and as they drink it she asks him questions about whatever problems are confronting her. They are generally questions like, "How can I get my boss to treat me more seriously?" or, "Where should I go on my vacation?" Then she listens to the answer, thanks the old man, and leaves.

What these examples illustrate is that all of these methods of communicating with your intuition work. The key is to choose a technique that works for you—or even create your own mental journey to unlock your intuition so it gives you answers and insights.

You can also get quick answers as you go through the day with other techniques. For example, sometimes I'll want an immediate yes-or-no decision. Should I trust a man I recently met at a party and make a small investment in his start-up project? Should I go to a business meeting or should I stay home and work on a project? Such questions come up for everyone dozens of times a day, and obviously you can't take the time to use an extended visualization to discover an answer. You need to make your decision immediately.

In such cases, I seek an answer to a question one of two ways, and sometimes I even get the answer before I have fully asked the question. It happens that fast. The first way I get an answer is by seeing it on a screen in my mind or listening for my little voice to give me a yes, no, or short message. I ask my question—or sometimes I just feel it without putting it into words—and then I wait for the answer to appear on the screen in whatever form it comes. Sometimes it will be a single word flashing on the screen, sometimes a color (green for yes, red for no, and yellow for not sure right now), and sometimes the word yes or no is re-sounding in my head like a beeper.

Other people tend to get messages directly from their body. For example, when they get a yes, they feel a slight quickening of their pulse, experience a vibration in their chest and stomach, and feel their heart beating faster. One associate uses his body like a pendulum. When his body sways forward and back ever so slightly, he knows it's saying yes; when it swings right and left, the answer is no; and when he sways in circles, he feels he isn't sure. The movements are so small that other people can't detect them, but he can feel them, and in an instant he knows what to do. Use whichever approach works best for you in a particular situation to tap into your own unconscious.

Three Steps to First-Rate Decision-Making

How should you make a decision when faced with difficult choices? There are several key methods, and in each case your intuition can help you perceive your options and make the right choices. Look for opportunities and signs that suggest a favorable result. Look for ways to expand your options so you have more and better possibilities to choose from. Look within to tap your feelings and tune in to what you really want, not what you think you want, feel you should want, or are pressured to want by others.

Step 1: Look for Opportunities and Signs

The idea of looking for opportunities and signs is not a new one. The Roman generals looked for signs and omens before going into battle, the Chinese searched for signs and omens to determine whether a couple should marry, and similar practices exist today. Many people report positive results following signs to help them make decisions.

Jerry had been feeling down after breaking up with his long-term girlfriend, who suddenly decided to marry someone else, when a friend called urging him to go to a networking party that night. But Jerry was in no mood to go out. Instead, after work he planned to go straight home, but on the way out he passed an announcement for the big networking event his friend had just told him about. For Jerry, the poster was like a sign that he should go to the event, so he called his friend to go with him. The result was that he met a woman who had just moved to town. They hit it off, began dating, and after a few months were engaged. What made this possible was Jerry's openness to these coincidences. First his friend's invitation to an event, then seeing the poster about that same event were signs that Jerry was to go to it. He followed them, led by his intuition that told him that this was a signal to go in that direction for positive results.

Follow the Signs to Opportunities

To take advantage of the windows of opportunity that may be open to you, follow these steps:

1) Make yourself aware of and pay attention to these signs when they appear.

   For example, if you need to make a decision, keep it firmly in mind and remind yourself that you are looking for clues or guidelines to help you make it.

2) Remember that these clues and signs come in many forms.

   For some the signs come in dreams, for others they are more concrete—the economy or world events. Still others get their signals from what people say, including chance remarks and comments while others respond to anomalous or unusual events. There is no one source. The point is to notice what has a resonance or congruence for you, what leads you to believe something offers a window of opportunity for you, what makes you feel intuitively that something is right for you, and to use the signs that have the most meaning.

3) When you do get a strong signal, investigate it to make sure it is valid and useful.

   Don't act impulsively. Sometimes we tune in to the wrong signal or misinterpret what seems to be a strong clue. Examine the signal in light of the other things you are experiencing and ask yourself, *Does this sign confirm other things that I am experiencing? Does it reinforce other things that might lead me to make this decision?* If the answer is yes, it is an indication that the signal is valid and that you can use it to guide you. If the answer is no because the sign seems inconsistent with everything else you are experiencing, investigate it further.

4) If you truly believe that a signal is valid, be ready to respond to it.

If you've learned to read and trust your intuition when you get a positive, good-to-go sign, the final step is moving ahead. It's like seeing your dream house and then acting to make an offer. You've got to be ready to act, though the difference between doing this and acting impulsively or rashly is having a clear signal to act. Otherwise, if the good-to-go signal is uncertain, such as a warning sign that causes you to waver, then that's when you should wait to check your signal and hold back until you have that clear sign that everything's good to go.

Step 2: Expand Your Options

In general, you can make better decisions when you have a number of desirable alternatives to choose from. Too many options can sometimes be confusing and can hinder decision making, but too few options can make you feel stuck if none of the options really appeal to you. In general though, you can make better decisions and break through logjams by looking for new possibilities and alternatives so you have more and better options from which to choose, increasing your chances of choosing and getting what you want.

Brainstorming to Find Alternatives

A good way to come up with options is by brainstorming. Here the focus is on how to apply brainstorming to decision making. Brainstorming is an ideal way to come up with new ideas because it helps you create alternatives. Alternatives aren't helpful when you are in an either/or situation in which you have no input, but where options are possible creative brainstorming can help you make better decisions.

Creating Inner Focus for Better Brainstorming

This exercise will help you to focus so that you can brainstorm ideas and alternatives most effectively. Initially, do it when you are alone and in a quiet place. With practice, you can achieve this state anywhere. It will help you tune out external influences.

Get in a calm, relaxed state with your eyes closed. Concentrate on focusing inward. Imagine that you are looking at something with a point in its center, such as a long deep hole, a tunnel, or a bull's-eye. As you gaze at it, project yourself into that central point. You feel totally directed, totally focused. That point is the only thing that exists in your consciousness.

Then, with your consciousness directed on that point, notice how you can turn the stimuli of the outer world on and off. To do this, continue focusing on this point; notice whatever sounds, smells, movements, or other sensations are around you. Pay attention to them for a moment. Next, turn your attention completely away, back to that center point. Again imagine that nothing else exists and turn off those external sounds, smells, movements, or other sensations.

Then, turn your attention back to the external world for a few minutes, then back to your inner world. Do this several times. Notice that you have the ability to shift your attention back and forth. You can be totally focused either outside or in as you choose.

Next, concentrate on holding your attention somewhere in the middle of the two worlds; aware of both your internal world and the external world. It's as if your awareness is on a fence and you can shift your focus from one side to the other, or sit right on the fence so you can experience both worlds simultaneously. Practice shifting your focus from one place to another—to the external world, to the middle between worlds, and to the internal world. Try moving gradually from world to world with a stop in the middle, then practice jumping your attention back and forth between the external and internal world. As you do, notice how your awareness and experience change and notice that it becomes easier and easier to shift your focus.

Now redirect your focus back to that center point and gradually release your attention. When you feel ready, return to the everyday world and open your eyes.

Generating Decision-Making Ideas

Individual (personal) brainstorming is the method most often used for decisionmaking. At the initial idea-generating stage you should:

1) Find a quiet, calm, relaxing place where you can tune out the influences of the external world.

2) Get into a receptive, responsive, inward-looking state of mind.

3) Let go of the logical-rational-critical-judgmental part of your mind.

4) Once in this receptive state, ask a triggering question. Be specific, but present your question in an open-ended way, such as, *In how many ways can I solve this particular problem?*

5) After you present your question remain centered, focused, and receptive. Let the ideas flow up and through you. Pay attention, but just observe or listen; don't try to guide or direct. At this stage accept whatever comes.

6) Record the responses so you don't lose them. Write them down or record them on tape. In some cases, you may receive additional ideas as you write or record. Don't inhibit them; just let them happen if or when they occur.

7) Keep the process going as long as you are readily coming up with ideas. When the ideas start slowing down, ask yourself, *Is there anything else?* Or ask a related question. Listen or observe to see if there are further ideas.

When you feel the process is complete, let go of this concentrated, focused-inward state and return to a more neutral or logical/rational state. For the next stage, use your logical-rational-critical-judgmental mind to review and assess the ideas you have come up with. One good way is to rate the ideas on a scale of zero to five to choose those you like the best, and then prioritize or choose the best one to make a selection of alternatives.

Step 3: Tap into Your Feelings and Tune into Your Real Desires

While expanding your options and alternatives can give you more choices when a limited selection is the problem, what do you do when you know the possibilities and you can't decide among them? Or what if your choices are limited to yes, no, or maybe? What if you don't have the time to get more information or work out the pros and cons logically? What if you find that additional information is further confusing you and weighing you down?

One way to break through the confusion, figure out what you really want, and make a quick decision is to tune in to your inner mind to learn what your unconscious desires are, or what your intuition thinks is best for you. Once you access it, your intuition can help you decide. It can break through the self-imposed barriers—fear statements such as "it won't work" and "I can't do it"—that you put up when faced with a difficult decision. The following techniques are designed to make you more sensitive to that inner voice or vision.

Pathways to Your Inner Feelings

It is important to realize that when you tune in to your intuition to determine what you really want, you can use many channels or pathways to access it. The key is to find those intuitive mechanisms that work best for you. As previously discussed, the four ways you may get intuitive information could be seeing, hearing, feeling, and sensing that you know something. The different channels or pathways this information may come could be automatic writing, automatic drawing, mental journeys, yes/no/maybe signals from your intuitive mind, or physical signals from your body.

Each person uses these pathways a little differently. One person may go on a mental journey by imagining him or herself going into a dark room and seeing the answer appear in the form of a film on the screen, while another may go into a workshop and see the answer on a computer monitor. Still another may go on a long mental journey into the mountains and seek the answer from a wise old man, and some may use more traditional shamanic imagery from tribal peoples. Similarly, there are a variety of ways to use automatic writing or to receive impulses from your brain and signals from your body. Different people prefer different techniques, and many people use multiple approaches depending on how they feel. The idea is to use what works best for you. Experiment with different methods until you find those you prefer.

The following exercises demonstrate how you can use these techniques to tap into your own intuitive unconscious to make a decision. Incidentally, although the focus of this chapter has been on decision making and problem solving, these techniques can readily be applied to many other situations as well, such as developing ideas for new projects.

Using Automatic Writing to Make Decisions

Automatic writing can help you get the insight you need to make the right decision or find the answer to a problem or question. While any form of writing—longhand, computer, or typewriter—is fine, when you are just starting you may find that longhand is more conducive to the process. It is easier to go off to a quiet, isolated place where you may feel a more direct connection with your thoughts. To set the stage create a comfortable writing environment that will help you get into a quiet, inner-focused state. You may want to dim the lights, light a candle, or put on some soft background music. Have your writing materials readily available.

When you're ready to begin, get calm and relaxed using a relaxation technique or even a repetitive physical exercise to get you into a trance-like state. Once in this relaxed, focused, receptive state you are ready to begin writing. If you have music on, turn it off so you can concentrate. Begin asking any questions about your decision. Be receptive to whatever comes, and immediately begin writing whatever comes to mind. You can ask your question however you wish. *What would I really like to do? Where should I go? What are my alternatives; which one do I really prefer? Which choice will be of the most benefit to me?*

Then write immediately and as quickly as possible. Even if the words don't make sense or come in single words or phrases rather than sentences, write them down. Don't think or analyze. You may find that you sometimes get random thoughts that jump around; just write them down as they come. Or the writing may become a direct line between your thoughts and the paper. You don't even hear your self-talk; instead you discover what you are thinking as you write or after the words are written. This latter state is ideal because your automatic writing is directly recording your inner consciousness. Sometimes, particularly when you are in this deeply focused state, you may feel the thoughts are coming to you from a spirit or guide, and that's fine, too. Whatever helps you access your inner truth will contribute to the process. However you get your answers, keep writing. When you have finished writing the answer to one question, ask another. Keep asking questions and writing the answers until the questions and responses stop and you feel the process is complete.

Then let go of this inner state and come back to ordinary consciousness. Review what you have written and interpret any words or phrases that are not immediately clear. What you have written should indicate the choice you want to make.

Automatic Drawing—Picture Your Decision

If you are better able to tap your intuitive mind through images and symbols than through words and thoughts, you may prefer automatic drawing to writing. The steps are much the same. Instead of writing down your answers, you will draw pictures and images and then interpret these images.

The steps are the same as for automatic writing. Set the stage by creating a comfortable environment. Have the drawing materials readily available. These can be very simple materials—paper or a notebook, and pencil or pen, or if you prefer, special drawing materials like sketch paper, crayons, colored pencils, magic markers, and so on. When you're ready to begin, get calm and relaxed using the same techniques described for automatic writing.

Then ask questions about your decision and be receptive to whatever comes. Begin drawing right away and draw as quickly as possible. The images may come in various forms—complete pictures, symbols, sometimes even words. Just draw whatever you see and don't think or analyze.

You may find that sometimes you are seeing pictures and drawing what you have seen after the fact. Or the drawing may become like a direct line for your thoughts—you see the images only as you are drawing them or after you have drawn them. The ideal is to seek this latter state because then your automatic drawing is directly recording your inner consciousness and you are more fully in this focused, concentrated inner state. Whatever helps you feel you are accessing your inner truth will contribute to the process. However you get your answers, keep drawing. When you have finished drawing the answer to one question, ask another. Keep asking questions and drawing what you see until the questions and responses stop and you feel complete with the process.

Let go of this inner state and come back to ordinary consciousness. Review what you have drawn and interpret any symbols or images that are unclear. Whatever you have drawn should indicate the choice you want to make.

Taking a Mental Journey to Reach Decisions

Mental journeys can take a variety of forms. In general, they involve taking a mental trip to a place where you will find the answer to your question. The journey itself helps you get into this deeper, focused, aware state. Once you arrive, the particular place you go or the person or guide or things you encounter there can help you find the answer. Each person's journey is personal. Use whatever images and interpretations of these images that work for you. The key is to get in touch with your inner knowledge, in whatever way works best for you. Here are two representative types of mental journeys. You can use these or feel free to create your own.

Technique 1: Asking a Counselor for Advice

This technique takes you to a workshop where you'll speak with an expert adviser or counselor who will know all the answers you need to know. Depending on your preference, this guide will appear as a person, animal, or spirit guide on the mental screen in your mind.

Begin by getting relaxed, and close your eyes. Imagine a special workshop or office in your house where you can go to find out whatever you want to know. It can be a special room anyplace in your house. Perhaps it is in the basement, attic, or garage. It might even be a special building on the roof or in the backyard.

Wherever it is, imagine your walk to go there. Go slowly and leisurely so you will be ready to go to work when you arrive. As you walk, notice what is around you. When you come to the door to this room, open it and go inside. As you enter, look around. There are all kinds of things there that you have been working on. There may be books and papers, things you have made, or projects you are working on. Sit down in the room. If you want to get your answer from an expert, just wait and he or she will come in the form of a person, animal, or spirit guide. Call on this expert to help you. In a moment, this expert will appear on your mental screen standing or sitting in front of you. Notice what the expert is like and say a few words of welcome. The expert may be someone you know, someone in the field you want help with, or he or she may just be someone who is very wise and knowledgeable.

Then state the question or problem you need to make a decision about. Ask for help in deciding among the alternatives. Listen as your counselor or adviser tells you what to do. He or she may tell you verbally or the answer may appear as a message on your mental screen. Continue to ask any more questions you may have and your counselor will reply. Again, wait for your answer. When you have no more questions, tell your counselor you are done and they will say goodbye and leave. Then turn off the screen in your mind and leave your workshop. Return to your house, and as you do, return to normal consciousness. Open your eyes.

Usually this process provides clear answers. If, however, your counselor has not provided answers or has asked you to wait, this probably means you don't have enough information or that the situation is still unclear. If this is the case, wait a few days and ask your questions again or try another technique to obtain more information. You may also need to get more information from external sources, such as other people, magazines, or books about the situation to help you make your decision.

Technique 2: Taking a Mental Journey to Find the Answer

This journey technique takes you to a distant setting to get your answer. It can take you any place, but some typical trips are to the top of a mountain to learn the answers from a wise old man or woman, to a pool of water where you will see the answer in the water, to a cave where you will meet power animals or teachers who can help you, to the clouds where you will encounter wise teachers or spiritual beings, and so forth. The following exercise is designed to let you choose where you want to go and who you want to meet when you get there to help you make your decision. You can use this technique in one of two ways. One is to read this description and use it to guide your experience in a general way, and the other is to record the journey on a recording device and play it back while you listen.

Begin by getting relaxed. Close your eyes. Then imagine yourself in the middle of a meadow. It is a beautiful sunny day and you are sitting under a shady tree. Now look around the meadow to decide where you want to go for help with your decision. If you look to the west, you can take a path down to the river or a lake. If you look to the north, you can follow a path that leads to a cave. If you look to the east, you can follow a path to a mountain, and you can walk up to the top of it. If you look to the south, you will see a very tall tree that leads up into the clouds, and if you wish, you can climb the tree to the clouds. Wherever you go you will feel very comfortable and very safe, and you will find your answers there.

Now, choose which path you want to follow: to the river or a lake, to the cave, to the mountaintop, or to the clouds. Begin walking. As you do, notice the scenery around you. You may notice lush green foliage or you may see flowers. You may hear birds singing. You may see some animals in the distance. Just notice whatever's there and feel comfortable and at ease as you walk on this beautiful day where the air is clear and warmed by the sun.

Now you are approaching your destination. If you are going to the water or the cave, notice the path is descending. Or if you are going to the mountain or up the tree to the clouds, notice the path is going up. Now see your destination and continue your walk. Once you are there, look around. You may see someone approach who will be your teacher or guide. Or you may see an animal who has come to help you. This is your power animal. Whoever approaches—person or animal—ask if they will be your teacher or guide or will show you to your teacher or guide.

Your teacher will welcome you and invite you to ask a question. After you ask it, listen or observe. You will get your answer. It may be in the form of words, or your teacher may take you somewhere, show you something, or ask you to look ahead of you to a place where you will see your answer revealed. Just be open and receptive to whatever comes, in whatever form. If you have additional questions, you can ask them after you get the answer to your first question.

Afterward, thank your teacher, who will lead you back to the entrance. Say goodbye. You will see the path you took. Return on it now. Go back to the meadow where you began your journey. Sit down under the tree again and gradually let go of the experience and return to your everyday consciousness.

Making Quick Decisions

For quick, everyday decisions you obviously can't take the time needed to go on mental journeys or have an ongoing dialogue with your expert. Instead you need a way to tap into your intuition quickly to get a rapid-fire answer to a question that needs only a simple yes, no, or maybe. If there are just a few alternatives, you want a quick signal to say this or that is best. This approach is particularly useful when you have to make a fast yes-or-no decision, or if you are feeling outside pressure to make a decision but feel some inner resistance. A quick intuitive response can help you make the choice and feel better about your decision. The following techniques are designed to provide you with some alternate ways of getting quick answers from your intuitive mind in the form of words, images, symbols, or from your body.

Getting Quick Yes, No, or Maybe Answers from Your Intuition

This technique, which uses words, images, or symbols, is designed to quickly tap into your inner intuition or feelings to get an immediate and clear yes, no, or maybe answer. To use this technique effectively, you either have to do some preliminary conditioning to get your mental screen ready to respond immediately, or you can look within to see what word, image, or symbol you used in similar situations and use it.

To get in touch with the feeling or sense you have when you must give a yes-or-no answer or make a quick, clear choice, take some time to get relaxed and comfortable and close your eyes. Then, in this very relaxed, comfortable state imagine you are going to be taking a truth test where you want to see your real feelings. Now ask yourself a series of questions to which you know the answer and can answer yes or no, or you can make a clear either/or choice. *Was I born in California? Did I go to school in New York? Is my favorite color red or blue?*

As you give each truthful answer, notice how you feel. Also, notice if you gave the answer as a word you heard, as a word you said in your mind, as an image you saw, or something you felt.

Now ask either those same questions or different questions, but this time answer untruthfully. Intentionally say the wrong answer or make the wrong choice. Again notice the feelings, images, and thoughts associated with the wrong answer. Reflect on the differences in how you felt. You will probably find that when you were saying something you really felt was true the feelings were much clearer and stronger. You had a sense of certainty. Perhaps the image of the word seemed brighter or the sound of the word in your mind seemed louder.

Now ask yourself a series of questions to which you don't have answers or haven't yet made a decision about. Ask your intuitive mind to give you the appropriate response. At first, each time you respond notice the feelings, images, and associations you experience with that yes, no, or maybe choice. Get a clear sense of what it is like to say yes, no, or to make a choice and be very firm in that decision.

Then speed up the process. Ask the questions faster and faster and give a quicker and quicker response. Don't pay conscious attention to the feelings, images, and thoughts associated with the act of saying yes, no, or making a choice. The goal is to respond so automatically and so intuitively that you don't have to think about your response anymore. Your feelings, images, and associations are all triggered at once as you respond, and you know immediately how you really feel on that gut or inner level. Finally, when you feel ready, stop asking questions and responding and return to the room.

Continue to practice this technique for about a week or until you feel that your yes-no quick choice response has become a part of your life. Also, try using this technique to get answers in everyday life. You'll find your answers will come more and more quickly and easier in whatever form they appear.

Getting Answers from Your Intuition

An alternate way to get yes, no, or maybe answers is by asking your body. In this way, you go past your conscious thoughts to your inner feelings, which are reflected in how your body reacts. As with the previous technique, to tune in to your intuitive mind you need some practice to train your responses until they become automatic. The difference here is that you are training your physical body rather than your mind to respond with cues. After you work with these physical movements, you can visualize them or replace them with a voice in your mind so you can pick up these cues anywhere. The following technique involves using your arm as a pendulum, or use another part or your whole body if you prefer.

To begin, place your elbow on a desk and hold your arm and hand up. Then move it around freely in all directions. Next, imagine that your arm is a truth meter. Sway your arm like a pendulum backward and forward, and as you do repeat the word, *yes … yes* to yourself again and again. This backward and forward motion means yes. Next, sway your arm to the right and left and as you do repeat the word, *no … no* to yourself again and again. This right to left motion means no. Finally, sway your arm in the free motion you started with. As you do, repeat the phrase *not sure* or *maybe* to yourself. Choose the phrase you prefer and repeat it again and again. This free-form motion means *not sure* or *maybe*.

To test that you have made the associations between yes, no, and maybe and your arm's motions, try asking a few yes-no questions that you know the answers to. Your arm should respond with the appropriate swaying motions. Once it does this consistently, you are ready to begin asking it for answers. As you become more practiced in using this technique so the bodily motions are truly automatic, you don't need to actually move your arm. You can imagine this movement in your mind's eye. Just ask your question and observe how your arm responds to get your answer. Later you can just ask your question and you will feel your body respond with a yes or no.

Some Tips on Asking Your Questions

In both of these techniques it's important to ask your questions in the right way so you tap into what you really feel. For example, don't ask, *What should I do?* because that implies outside pressure influencing your decision. Instead, ask your question in a more neutral or feeling way. For example, *Which do I really feel best about doing?* or *Which do I personally prefer?*

If you get a lot of maybes to a question, it may be that you need more information. If that is the case, just ask your question at a later time. Or the uncertain response may be because you are not asking the question clearly or because outside influences or your beliefs about what to do or think are getting in the way. To find out, ask, *Is my question unclear? Is someone else influencing my answer? Are my beliefs or thoughts getting in the way?* If this is the case, clarify or reframe your question or push your conscious thoughts and feelings aside so you can listen to your inner self.

Making an Important Decision

The following techniques are methods for making an important decision or getting answers to questions you have. As these techniques require you to take time to be with yourself quietly, I recommend using them only occasionally and using the quick decision methods on an everyday basis. If you find you have more of an affinity to one of these techniques than the others, use that. Or vary the techniques you use depending on the situation and what feels right at the time. For all of these techniques find a place where you can get relaxed and comfortable. Close your eyes if you like.

Making the Write Decision

In this technique, you'll use automatic writing to learn what you need to know. To set the stage, have paper and pencil available or get in front of your computer, laptop, or tablet so you can immediately begin to type. Perhaps use a notebook or Word document to keep track of your communications on a regular basis. It also helps to create a comfortable writing environment that will help to alter your consciousness. For instance, use candles or dim lighting, and if you like, put on some background music—preferably something soft and easy to listen to.

Then, use a relaxation technique to alter your state of consciousness, such as concentrating on your breathing or focusing on a single word like *om* or *relax*. Once you feel spacey, you are ready to begin writing. Turn off any music because you need quiet to concentrate.

Now ask any questions about your decision mentally or write them down. *What should I do? What is in my best interest? What would I like to do? What are my alternatives? Which alternatives would I prefer?* And so on.

Then wait for your answer. It may come to you as a voice in your head, or it may seem like a communication from a spirit guide, or a being with a personality. Either way, write down your answer as it comes. Don't think or analyze, just write. Keep asking questions and recording answers until the questions and responses stop. Finally, review what you have written. The course you want to take should be clear.

Asking Your Counselor for Advice

In this technique, you'll imagine a TV or computer screen in your mind to contact an expert counselor or spirit guide who knows all the answers. Imagine that you have a special place in your house where you can go to find out whatever you want to know. It may be in the attic or basement, perhaps it is a new addition in the garage, or maybe it used to be a bedroom. Wherever it is, imagine yourself going there and take your time getting there. Notice what is around you as you walk, and when you are ready, open the door and go inside. As you enter, look around. There may be paintings on the walls, piles of papers, equipment, and whatever else is normally in the room. Then, at the far wall you notice a long desk, and above it a large TV or computer screen with numerous gadgets and buttons to press. Just press a button and you can see a movie of your own experiences on this screen.

Now, to work on resolving some problem or getting advice, press the button and you'll see the situation that you want to resolve unfold on the screen. Or you may see the question you want to ask appear. Once the problem or question is clear, you can seek a solution or answer. To obtain this, press a button to stop the movie and press another to summon your counselor or spirit guide. He or she will appear on the screen with advice for you. Your counselor or guide may be someone you know or could just look like someone very knowledgeable. Whoever it is, welcome your counselor and ask for help. Tell him or her what is wrong and ask for advice on what to do or say to resolve matters.

Listen as your counselor tells you what to do. If the answer is simple, he or she will reply briefly, or your counselor may ask you to press a button on your console so you can see the solution. Then, the action you can take will appear on the screen.

If you have more questions, continue to ask them and your counselor will reply. Again, wait for your answer in whatever form it comes. When you have no more questions, tell your counselor you are done and their image will disappear from the screen. Then turn off your TV or computer console and leave this room. Return to the regular part of your house, and as you do, return to normal consciousness and open your eyes. Usually you will have clear answers as a result of this process. However, if your counselor has no answers or asks you to wait, this means you don't have enough information or the situation is unclear. If so, perhaps wait a few days and ask your questions again, or use some of the other techniques described in this book to obtain more information or increase your confidence so you are in a better position to take action.

Taking a Journey to Find the Answer

In this technique you'll take a journey up to the top of a mountain to learn your answers from the wise man or woman of the mountain. To take this journey you need to be very relaxed and comfortable. You can best use this technique in two ways. One way is to read this description first and use it to guide your experience in a general way. The other is to record the journey on a recording device and play it back while you listen. The following guide uses a wise man. Substitute a wise woman if you prefer.

This journey begins in the midst of a beautiful meadow. See yourself there surrounded by lush green foliage. The air is clear and warmed by the sun. Nearby you hear the subtle buzz of bees and the chatter of birds. Off in the distance you see a large mountain and walk toward it. As you walk, notice the tiny flowers. Little mushrooms pop up in the shade of trees. You can feel the carpet of moss beneath your feet. Cows grazing on the hillside moo softly.

As you walk toward the mountain the trees begin to thin out and you pass patches of grassland. The wind feels stronger and cooler. Now you pass a small stream. Sit down for a moment. Let your feet dangle in the stream. Feel the water move past them. It's so relaxing. You feel very peaceful. Now sit very still and listen. Notice the infinite variety of movements around you. Dragonflies make darting passes as they skim the stream. A crab crawls out from under a stone seeking a better place to hide. Tadpoles swim by, and above your head birds fly from perch to perch. Squirrels race up a tree. Insects balance themselves on blades of grass. Nearby, a deer stands quietly watching. Sit on a large rock and look around you. What else do you see?

Now go on, and as you walk uphill, note that the trees give way to bushes. You come to a clearing and look down on the meadow and valley below. Notice how far away it seems—like another world. As you climb higher and higher, notice how the air begins to cool. Yet the sun shines on you directly and warms you. As you climb, experience a sense of clarity and self-understanding as you get farther and farther away from the things that usually concern you. It is as if you are leaving the world and all its cares behind. Realizing this, you feel an intense sense of peace.

Now you come near the top of the mountain. At the top, there is a small hut made of intricately carved wood. The windows and doorways are hung with mirrors and small objects that flash and shine in the light. This is where the wise man of the mountain lives. He is said to know about everything. You approach the cabin. As you do, think of the questions you wish to have answered. Think of the decision you have to make and select your most important question to ask first. With your question clearly in mind, go up to the door and knock three times. The wise man will answer. As he opens the door he asks, "What question do you bring?" In response, look him in the eyes and clearly state your question. As you do, observe him closely. Notice his eyes and the way he is dressed. He looks like a seer who knows the answers to all things. Then he invites you into his cabin to share tea. As you drink it, he tells you the answer to your question. Listen as he answers your question. If you have additional questions, ask them after he finishes his answer. Afterward thank him for his answers. Talk of other things if you like and stay as long as you wish. When you say goodbye, go back down the mountain as you came and return to the meadow where you began your journey.

Chapter Thirteen

∾

Making GWYW Techniques
a Regular Part of Your Life

So now you're ready to make the GWYW techniques described in the previous chapters a regular part of your life. Feel free to take the principles underlying these techniques and use them to modify and adapt these methods as you like, depending on your own situation, personality, behavior style, previous experiences, and other factors. For everyone is different and has different goals, everyday challenges, and systems of meaning. So if you want to use another image or procedure to achieve a desired result, by all means do so. And feel confident you can make these work for you. A key is to believe in yourself and your ability to do it and then practice on a regular basis until, like developing any habit, they become part of you.

As long as you follow the basic principles and use these techniques fairly regularly (about twenty minutes or more a day), these techniques will work. The key is learning to relax, directing your intuitive abilities to some goal, and being confident you have the power to achieve what you want. Then, trust your intuitive powers and let them operate freely so they are not restricted or held back by your logical mind. The techniques in this book will help you channel and guide this power, but feel free to use other images and procedures to achieve the same end. For once you create the open channel, your intuitive abilities will provide you with the needed insights and receptivity to guide you. No matter what you want to achieve in your work, business, or personal life, no matter how you seek to enrich your life, you can direct your intuitive powers to help you achieve your goals. Just concentrate on creating what you want to happen and soon you'll find that it will occur or that your work and life situation generally will change in positive ways.

Just watch. Positive things will begin to happen more frequently at work and at home. Even if you don't ask for these things specifically, they will come because working with your inner knowing and creative powers releases streams of constructive, positive energy. And when you mobilize your inner forces in this positive way that's what you will get back. To help you notice the change, keep a list of the goals you have achieved or a regular journal to chart each day. You might even start a daily or weekly blog where you describe what you have achieved and the techniques you used along the way. In turn, keeping this list, journal, or blog will make the things you want happen even faster because the act of writing down your experiences will make you more open and aware.

Work on applying these GWYW techniques and you'll find both your work and personal life transforming for the better. Decide what you want, work with the processes described in this book, and you're on your way to getting what you want.

So now…begin. You have the intuitive abilities within you to mold and shape whatever you want!

For information on workshops, seminars, and training programs contact Gini Graham Scott at:

Changemakers
3527 Mt. Diablo Blvd., #273
Lafayette, CA 94549
(925) 385-0608
changemakers@pacbell.net
Her websites are:
www.changemakerspublishingandwriting.com
or
www.ginigrahamscott.com

To Write to the Author

If you wish to contact the author or would like more information about this book, please write to the author in care of Llewellyn Worldwide Ltd. and we will forward your request. Both the author and publisher appreciate hearing from you and learning of your enjoyment of this book and how it has helped you. Llewellyn Worldwide Ltd. cannot guarantee that every letter written to the author can be answered, but all will be forwarded. Please write to:

Gini Graham Scott, PhD
℅ Llewellyn Worldwide
2143 Wooddale Drive
Woodbury, MN 55125-2989

Please enclose a self-addressed stamped envelope for reply,
or $1.00 to cover costs. If outside the U.S.A., enclose
an international postal reply coupon.

Many of Llewellyn's authors have websites with additional information and resources. For more information, please visit our website at
http://www.llewellyn.com

Clearing Clutter
Physical, Mental, and Spiritual
ALEXANDRA CHAURAN

Clutter brings stress to our lives. Whether it's in our home, cubicle, mind, life, or spirit, it's hard to be clearheaded and focused with so much *stuff* stressing us out. *Clearing Clutter* shows you how to clear clutter in all its forms: physical, mental, and spiritual. Feng shui is used when talking about clearing space in your home and creating a good flow of energy. Meditation is used to clear and focus our minds and thoughts and connect to spirit. Organizing and minimizing the physical objects around us brings positivity to each aspect of our lives.

978-0-7387-4227-4, 216 pp., 5 ³/₁₆ x 8   **$15.99**

Finding
Your Center,
Getting in the Flow,
&
Creating the Life You Desire

The Art of Bliss

Tess Whitehurst

Author of *Magical Housekeeping*

The Art of Bliss
Finding Your Center, Getting in the Flow,
and Creating the Life You Desire
TESS WHITEHURST

Bring harmony and balance to every area of your life with this gentle, loving guide to beautiful living and personal evolution.

Popular author Tess Whitehurst offers a totally unique and fun magical system for reconnecting with your bliss, also known as your life force energy. Weaving together the I Ching, feng shui, and a sprinkling of magic, she teaches you to activate your nine life keys for success and happiness. Become attuned to the areas of serenity, life path, synchronicity, creativity, romance, radiance, prosperity, harmony, and synergy—and awaken each with affirmations, breathwork, prayer, meditation, smudging, rituals, and many more energetically potent tools.

978-0-7387-3196-4, 312 pp., 5 ³⁄₁₆ x 8   **$16.99**

Becoming
your
Best Self

The Guide to Clarity, Inspiration and Joy

Sara
Wiseman

"Intuition is our most natural way of knowing. This book helps you return to
innate clarity and flow with easy, commonsense tips and insights. It guides you
into your truest self and life."
—Penney Peirce, author of *Frequency* and *The Intuitive Way*

Becoming Your Best Self
The Guide to Clarity, Inspiration and Joy
SARA WISEMAN

At its core, intuition is a spiritual act, says Sara Wiseman, and once you understand this simple concept, psychic awakening is a given. To this end, she teaches a direct connection with the Divine that will raise your vibration, heal your heart, allow instant access to cosmic information—and transform your life in the process.

Using elegantly simple teachings and step-by-step exercises, Wiseman makes it possible for students at all levels to experience their own psychic awakening. Readers will learn a variety of life-enhancing skills, from attracting a soul mate to healing relationships through space and time to communicating with Divine guides, angels, and loved ones in spirit.

978-0-7387-2794-3, 264 pp., 6 x 9   **$16.95**

"An amazing book that gives enlightened awareness of the greatness within you.
If you're ready to change your life, *The Steady Way to Greatness* is a must-read."
—MELISSA ALVAREZ, author of *365 Ways to Raise Your Frequency*

The
Steady
Way to
Greatness

Liberate Your Intuitive Potential
& Manifest Your Heartfelt Desires

MELANIE BARNUM

The Steady Way to Greatness
Liberate Your Intuitive Potential
& Manifest Your Heartfelt Desires
Melanie Barnum

Use intuition and psychic development to master the law of attraction and manifest the life you truly desire. *The Steady Way to Greatness* is a new and groundbreaking combination of manifestation and intuition for success in career, finances, love, relationships, spirituality, and more. Organized into a progression of fifty-two weekly practices, this guide includes affirmations and other exercises designed to increase confidence, discover the power of goal setting, and expose the magnificence that resides within.

Intuitive counselor Melanie Barnum is the perfect guide to help you reach your true potential. The stories and exercises she includes are designed for:

- Exploring positive and negative attitudes
- Opening to intuitive senses
- Identifying strengths
- Creating and living your dream life

978-0-7387-3835-2, 264 pp., 6 x 9   **$15.99**

Adrian Calabrese, Ph.D.

How to Get Everything You Ever Wanted

Complete Guide to Using Your Psychic Common Sense

How to Get Everything You Ever Wanted
Complete Guide to Using Your
Psychic Common Sense
ADRIAN CALABRESE

Love, money, cars, homes, even good health! Learn how you can begin immediately to manifest everything you want or need with the step-by-step approach presented by Dr. Calabrese. Hundreds of her clients and students have achieved outstanding practical results using the methods in this book, which includes an interactive workbook section in each chapter.

978-1-56718-119-7, 288 pp., 7 ½ x 9 ⅛   **$16.95**

Ana
Holub

Forgive
and Be
Free

A Step-by-Step Guide
to Release, Healing
& Higher Consciousness

"*Forgive and Be Free* . . . gives you the deep understanding and
step-by-step tools you need to be emotionally healthy, happy, and
compassionate with yourself and others. Highly recommended!"
—Colin Tipping, author of *Radical Forgiveness*

Forgive and Be Free
A Step-by-Step Guide to Release,
Healing & Higher Consciousness
ANA HOLUB

Forgiveness will heal you, free you, and catapult your life into a completely new territory of blessings and miracles. This comprehensive guide will help make your life more creative, abundant, and compassionate.

Forgive and Be Free offers an easy, step-by-step approach to forgiveness with the spiritual foundation that is necessary for ultimate healing. There are many reasons to forgive, and when you do, you'll find peace of mind, incredible joy, and stronger love. With personal stories, case histories, and hands-on exercises, author Ana Holub will bring you safely through emotional hardships and into serenity. Learn to offer your own forgiveness, challenge your courage to meet your past with compassion, and discover the ecstatic bliss of release, healing, and higher consciousness.

978-0-7387-3617-4, 288 pp., 5³/₁₆ x 8　　　　　　　　　　**$16.99**

COSMIC

ANNE JIRSCH

"Jirsch has taken complicated and abstract ideas and turned them into user-friendly concepts and techniques. The results will be life changing!"
—Paul McKenna, best-selling author of *Change Your Life in 7 Days*

How to Harness

the Invisible Power

Around You to

Transform Your Life

ENERGY

Cosmic Energy
How to Harness the Invisible Power
Around You to Transform Your Life
Anne Jirsch

Some people seem to lead a charmed life—they get what they want, they're in the right place at the right time, and even when they experience setbacks, they land on their feet. They're not just lucky—they're attuned to their cosmic energy.

Renowned psychic Anne Jirsch teaches readers how to connect with the flow of the universe to dramatically improve their lives. Using current studies, client examples, and personal stories, she explains a variety of highly effective techniques, from visualization and manifesting to working with etheric energy and thought field therapy.

Once the reader understands the basics of cosmic energy, Jirsch reveals how they can use the knowledge to improve their relationships, health, career, and finances.

978-0-7387-2125-5, 264 pp., 6 x 9   **$16.95**

Use the Vibration of Language
to Manifest the Life You Desire

the Energy of Words

MICHELLE ARBEAU

Foreword by **Marie D. Jones**, author of
11:11 The Time Prompt Phenomenon

The Energy of Words
Use the Vibration of Language
to Manifest the Life You Desire
MICHELLE ARBEAU

Manifest the life you truly desire with *The Energy of Words*. Choose the most powerful words and let the secret energy of language attract joy and abundance into your life!

Join internationally renowned numerologist Michelle Arbeau as she shows you how to determine your top ten power words; how to calculate the vibration of a word through the language of numbers; practical tips for positivity; the top one hundred positive and negative words; and stories of celebrities who have successfully worked with the power of words.

Negative words are energetic junk food. We can't manifest our desires if we're using words of lack and doubt. Learn how to eliminate negative vocabulary and replace it with positive personalized language that will transform your life into one of fulfillment and gratitude.

978-0-7387-3664-8, 312 pp., 5³⁄₁₆ x 8   **$15.99**
